BEHOLD THE MAN: A STUDY
OF THE FOURTH GOSPEL

Other books by Nathaniel Micklem

BEHOLD THE MAN: A STUDY OF THE FOURTH GOSPEL

by

NATHANIEL MICKLEM

*Sometime Principal of
Mansfield College, Oxford*

"I am accustomed to say that
this gospel affords the key to
open the door to other
gospels"

JOHN CALVIN

1969

GEOFFREY BLES · LONDON

SBN: 7138 0229 4

Printed in Great Britain
by Cox & Wyman Ltd, Fakenham

Published by
GEOFFREY BLES LTD
52 Doughty Street, London, W.C.1
33 York Street, Sydney
353 Elizabeth Street, Melbourne
246 Queen Street, Brisbane
CML Building, King William Street, Adelaide
Lake Road, Northcote, Auckland
100 Lesmill Road, Don Mills, Ontario
P.O. Box 8879, Johannesburg
P.O. Box 834, Cape Town
P.O. Box 2800, Salisbury, Rhodesia

CONTENTS

PREFACE

ANY addition to the avalanche of books now being published needs an apology, but this book more than most, for its subject is the Fourth Gospel upon which in the last fifty years many learned and improving treatises have been written. These in the main, apart from devotional and uncritical works, have been concerned either with "Johannine theology" or with the relation of the Fourth to the first three Gospels. My interest, on the other hand, is exclusively historical.

If I openly declare from the first that my own book rests upon guess-work, my admission will tend to alienate all potential readers, especially those non-professional readers who will say that, when it comes to the Gospels, it is facts they want, not speculations. Professional scholars, on the other hand, will be more wary or more tolerant being very conscious that guessing, though usually called by a politer name, is the way by which scholarship usually advances. The scholar espouses an hypothesis, which is an urbane name for a guess, tries how it will work out, and, if it prove convincing to him, will commend it to the judgement of his fellow-scholars. I have taken to myself such an hypothesis or guess, but mine differs from a purely academic thesis not only because I judge it to be of interest to all modern readers of the Bible, but also because any educated person may properly express an opinion on it.

Generally and on good grounds it is held that, whatever be the theological or religious value of the Fourth Gospel, it is not historical in the same sense as the first three, the Synoptics, as they are called. With this opinion up to a point I fully concur; indeed, as will be seen, I take a very radical view of the non-historical character of the Fourth Gospel as we have received it; yet as a daring paradox (*ingens et laetum paradoxon*) I write to elaborate the very opposite view, namely, that of all the Gospels the Fourth is the most historical.

7

The Germans make a distinction, which cannot be represented by English words, between *historisch* and *geschichtlich*. The difference is akin to that drawn by Edmund Spenser in his letter to Sir Walter Raleigh between historiographer and poet: "for an Historiographer discourseth of affayres orderly as they were donne, accounting as well the times as the actions, but a Poet thrusteth into the middest, even where it most concerneth him, and there recoursing to the thinges forepaste, and divining the thinges to come, maketh a pleasing Analysis of all". Luke claims to be historiographer, John was poet. But the poet, so his insight be true, comes nearer than can the historiographer to reveal the atmosphere, the colour, the chiaroscuro, the fullness, the real meaning of the event or saying which he records. Boris Pasternak in his *Essay in Autobiography* says, "It is not only true that music needs to be more than itself if it is to mean anything, but that everything in the world must surpass itself in order to be itself"*. Thus the sayings of Jesus must surpass themselves in order to be themselves. To put the matter in epigrammatic form, the Synoptists tell us what Jesus said; John tells us what Jesus never said but what he was always saying.

Before I declare my guess, I will state my presuppositions.

1. Even though in the Synoptists we find or suspect a distortion of oral tradition here and there, a heightening of the miraculous in the supposed interests of piety and the intrusion of elements from early Christian theology, we are still left with a clear picture of the kind of way in which Jesus taught and the kind of things he did. There is a superb objectivity about the writing of these evangelists: Jesus said this, he did that; there is no comment. The Synoptists are historical in a sense in which John is not. But this very objectivity is a weakness from another point of view. We are usually left to guess (for we are rarely told) the context in which Jesus said this or that; we are given little idea of what it was to see Jesus and to hear him, of the impression he made, of the atmosphere of strain which he inevitably created.

2. "The basic tradition on which the evangelist is working", writes C. H. Dodd of the Fourth Gospel, "was shaped, it appears, in a Jewish-Christian environment still in touch with the synagogue, in Palestine, at a relatively early date, at any rate before the

* English Translation p. 49.

8

rebellion of A.D. 66".* There is much circumstantial detail in this gospel which no one would have wanted to invent; yet its author sometimes makes mistakes, as when he supposes that the high priest was elected annually (XI. 51). I have, further, allowed myself to accept the established tradition that behind the Fourth Gospel (but how far behind we cannot say) lie the reminiscences, possibly in writing,† of an aged apostle, who is to be identified with "the disciple whom Jesus loved", the disciple who was an acquaintance of the high priest in Jerusalem. Indeed, in so far as my guess shall prove convincing, I shall afford support for the old tradition. This putative eye-witness behind the Gospel I shall, except when there is no possibility of confusion, always call "John I".

3. In distinction from the Synoptic Gospels which are compilations, the fourth is a literary composition of the poet or theologian or editor whom for brevity and convenience I shall always refer to as "John II". He drew, it may be, upon many sources of tradition, but his primary source I take to be the reminiscences of John I. The whole Gospel from first to last is a piece of Johannine writing; by Johannine, wherever the word occurs, I mean the language, style and theology of the editor, and wherever I speak of the editor I mean John II. My book is an attempt to discover John I behind John II.

4. John II, as I call him, was a theologian, a poet, a man of profound religious insight, of "a powerful and independent mind", but, I maintain, he was not a novelist. He relates incidents which, we feel sure, cannot have occurred precisely as he narrates them; he records sayings of Jesus which we can hardly ever take to be the words Jesus actually spoke; he intersperses his own comments as if they were the words of Jesus, but it is my (frankly indemonstrable) contention that he never invented an incident out of his own imagination, and had usually an historical basis for the sayings of Jesus which he records. Modern critical commentators have constantly implied, though they have never openly admitted, that John II had the gifts and the imagination of a novelist. Herein, I feel confident, they are mistaken. "If, as I suppose, John II also wrote the first epistle, then he was faced with an incipient

---

* *Historical Tradition in the Fourth Gospel,* p. 226.
† *v.* XXI. 24.

9

Docetism. He would have laid himself open to devastating riposte if he had deliberately introduced any element of fiction into his story."*

5. The picture of Jesus which I suppose most ordinary readers of the first three Gospels to draw for themselves is that of a great teacher with strange gifts of healing. So far as it goes, this no doubt is accurate; a different but not discordant picture of him comes from the one New Testament writer who was certainly his contemporary, and who, if he never saw Jesus, at least knew all about him from Peter and others of his circle. Paul says nothing, or next to nothing, of the teaching or "miracles" of Jesus, but he speaks constantly of "the Spirit" and of what it means "to walk by the Spirit"; this Spirit, as he tells us, is the Spirit of Jesus himself. From Paul we know very well, then, what manner of man will be the christlike person; we know the character of Jesus. But, further, Paul uses about Jesus language that seems to us extravagant, fantastic, mythological, representing him as the Second Adam, the pre-existent Son of God or the very Author of Creation. I am as little concerned here with the theology of Paul as with the theology of John II, but how could Paul who was a strict Jew, a scholar and a thinker use such astonishing language about any contemporary human being? It is quite obvious from these considerations that Jesus must have been a most extra-ordinary person.

These, then, are my presuppositions, first, that the Synoptists in spite of errors give us an objective, reliable, historical picture of the way Jesus taught and of the kind of things he did; second, that behind the Fourth Gospel there lie the authentic reminiscences of the eyewitness, whom I call John I; third, that the Fourth Gospel is so suffused and interpenetrated with the style and theology of John II that, till we come to the Passion narrative, it cannot be treated as giving us authentic history; fourth, that John II was not an imaginative writer with the gifts and calling of a novelist; fifth, that the teaching and theology of Paul imply that Jesus must have been a most extraordinary person.

I start from these presuppositions; my guess or hypothesis is that it is possible with varying degrees of assurance to find John I behind John II, and that the picture of Jesus which emerges from

* Dr George Caird in a letter to me.

the attempt to work out this hypothesis is not merely supplementary to that given in the Synoptic Gospels but is also in a strict sense more historical than they.

From readers of superior orthodoxy I lay myself wide open to the charge that I have presumed to rationalise the most spiritual of the Gospels. I think that is precisely what I have done, for I believe that Jesus of Nazareth was a real human being. This must not be taken to mean that I am interested to repudiate or 'deny' the many wonderful titles which Christian piety and theology have ascribed to him, but I keep to the Augustinian principle, *per Jesum ad Christum*, through Jesus to the Christ. In longer words, our theology is myth and phantasy unless it arise out of sober history. Resting upon the presuppositions which I have expounded I have attempted in this book to elucidate what I think may well have happened and what Jesus may well have said, or even must have said, to account for the Fourth Gospel which explicitly claims to be no novelist's reconstruction but a record of what actually occurred.

Traditional Christians will not have relished my earlier observation that Jesus must have been a most extraordinary person, for they read the Gospels in the light of the theology of Paul or John II or Calvin or Aquinas. These theologies may be proper conclusions to be reached *in the end*, but one who *starts* reading the Gospels in the light of any of these christologies will never see Jesus as a real human being. The picture that emerges from my study is of a Jesus completely human and yet of a loneliness and majesty only suggested in the other Gospels.

I have not treated of John II's prologue, regarding it as the worst introduction to the study of the historic Jesus as it is an incomparable exposition of his real significance. I have omitted an exposition of the resurrection narratives, for, though the abiding Gospel of the Christians is summed in the phrase "Jesus and the Resurrection", the whole purpose of my book is through this theological Gospel to see Jesus as the eyewitness saw him up to the time of his crucifixion.

An important element in the theology of John II, which dominates his treatment of his material is his doctrine of the Spirit. Much that Jesus said and did during his short life-span on earth the disciples at the time did not understand. The significance of "the

11

Triumphal Entry", for instance, only dawned upon them when he was "glorified", and "the Spirit of truth" was come (XII. 16). It was the function of the Spirit, which "did not speak of itself", to interpret the tradition, to expound the real meaning of the life that had been lived and the words that had been spoken (XVI. 13–15). An illustration may be taken from another book. In a parable (Luke XII. 39) Jesus said that, had the householder known at what hour the thief would come, he would not have allowed his house to be dug through. In Rev. III. 3 the risen Jesus says, "I will come as a thief" and, again, in Rev. XVI. 15, "behold, I come as a thief". The author, we may be sure, would never have invented the comparison between Jesus and a thief! He is expounding what the parable really meant. This is precisely in the style or method of John II in his "spiritual Gospel". From our modern critical-historical point of view he reports inaccurately, but he does not misrepresent; he sets forth the deeper truth, the ultimate significance of the words and deeds of Jesus as these came to be understood when "the Spirit" had been given. Not questioning John II's interpretation I have been concerned throughout to ask what Jesus must have said or done to give rise to John's exposition.

In the case of "miracles" such as the feeding of the five thousand or the walking on the water I have ventured with due hesitation to suggest what, as I suppose, may actually have occurred. It is impossible to determine whether the "miraculous" element in these stories comes from the interpretative imagination of John II or is part of the reminiscences of John I. It is entirely possible that John I, a man of the first century, would have seen as miraculous that which we with our modern scientific education would see in another light, and it may be deemed improbable that John II would have manufactured a miracle out of a story that reached him in another form. In these cases, then, I am asking what really happened rather than claiming to distinguish between the testimony of John I and the theological outlook of John II.

I have had the gravest hesitation in ascribing to Jesus any words not directly recorded of him, but it would be very tedious if I had written again and again, "Jesus may, or must, have said in effect or in substance . . ." whatever it might be. In my exposition I have deliberately and even painfully avoided the splendid, hieratic language of our Authorised Version, using very colloquial speech.

12

My one concern has been to see and depict the real Jesus of history behind the stylised, theological and devotional language of John II. I am most grateful to Canon Phillips for permission to print here his admirable translation, but it must not be inferred from this that he is committed to any of my speculations.

I have freely admitted that my book rests upon guessing, but it is not wild guessing. My guess concerning any particular passage may seem quite unconvincing to the reader, as taken by itself it does to me, but if the reader will follow me to the end, he will, I think, find the cumulative effect of my exposition overwhelmingly impressive, though never a matter of demonstration. He will come, I think, to see Jesus with new eyes.

My *apologia* is nearly at an end. I am sure that the enterprise of this book should be attempted. The task must be undertaken by one who is aware of the methods and findings of scholarship in the field of the New Testament; but no professional scholar can be expected to make himself so vulnerable to attack of fellow-professionals at every point; he cannot so openly admit that he is guessing. It is now many years since I slipped out of the world of scholarship and many more years since I had any claim to be regarded as a New Testament scholar, but I know in general how a scholar must set to work, and I am, as I think, sufficiently acquainted with the findings of scholars in respect of the Fourth Gospel; I have therefore a defensible standpoint from which to approach my question and no reputation to put at hazard in my attempt to answer it.

In the preparation of my book I have received the unstinted help of two friends to whom my warmest thanks are due. The Rev. John Wilding of Oxford has given scrupulous and meticulous attention to my typescript, made many significant suggestions and called my attention to other writers. Dr George Caird in spite of immense pressure of work has found time to read my typescript and write me many notes giving me freedom to make use of them. Neither of these friends is in any way committed to my opinions or, as I might better call them, my tentative suggestions.

Perhaps a word of autobiography may be permitted in conclusion. Like many others, as I suppose, I had for some time been reading (and perhaps avoiding) the Fourth Gospel with the feeling, "this is wonderful, this is beautiful, this may be spiritually true, but it didn't happen". Rereading the Gospel not long ago it came to me unexpectedly and even suddenly that with a little literary ingenuity and a modicum of common sense I could often guess with some degree of assurance what *must* have happened, what Jesus *must* have said that the evangelist has reported in his own religious terms. I hope that any reader, troubled as I have been by this Fourth Gospel, may have the patience to read these pages, for I seem to myself almost to have discovered a Fifth Gospel emerging from the Fourth.

N.M.

THE GOSPEL
OF JOHN

In the translation by
J. B. Phillips

CHAPTER I

Prologue

AT the beginning God expressed himself. That personal expres-   *1*
sion, that word, was with God, and was God, and he existed with   *2*
God from the beginning. All creation took place through him,   *3*
and none took place without him. In him appeared life and this   *4*
life was the light of mankind. The light still shines in the darkness   *5*
and the darkness has never put it out.

The gospel's beginning on earth

A man called John was sent by God as a witness to the light,   *6, 7*
so that any man who heard his testimony might believe in the
light. This man was not himself the light: he was sent simply as   *8*
a personal witness to that light.

That was the true light which shines upon every man as he   *9*
comes into the world. He came into the world – the world he had   *10*
created – and the world failed to recognise him. He came into his   *11*
own creation, and his own people would not accept him. Yet   *12*
wherever men did accept him he gave them the power to become
sons of God. These were the men who truly believed in him, and   *13*
their birth depended not on the course of nature nor on any im-
pulse or plan of man, but on God.

So the word of God became a human being and lived among   *14*
us. We saw his splendour (the splendour as of a father's only son),
full of grace and truth. And it was about him that John stood up   *15*
and testified, exclaiming: "Here is the one I was speaking about
when I said that although he would come after me he would
always be in front of me; for he existed before I was born!"
Indeed, every one of us has shared in his riches – there is a grace   *16*
in our lives because of his grace. For while the Law was given by   *17*
Moses, love and truth came through Jesus Christ. It is true that no   *18*
one has ever seen God at any time. Yet the divine and only Son,

who lives in the closest intimacy with the Father, has made him known.

John's witness

19 This then is the testimony of John, when the Jews sent priests
20 and Levites to ask him who he was. He admitted with complete candour, "I am not Christ."

21 So they asked him, "Who are you then? Are you Elijah?"
"No, I am not," he replied.
"Are you the Prophet?"
"No," he replied.

22 "Well, then," they asked again, "who are you? We want to give an answer to the people who sent us. What would you call yourself?"

23 "I am a voice shouting in the desert, 'Make straight the way of the Lord!' as Isaiah the prophet said."

24, 25 Now some of the Pharisees had been sent to John, and they questioned him, "What is the reason, then, for your baptising people if you are not Christ and not Elijah and not the Prophet?"

26 To which John returned, "I do baptise – with water. But some-
27 where among you stands a man you do not know. He comes after
28 me, it is true, but I am not fit to undo his shoes!" (All this happened in the Bethany on the far side of the Jordan where the baptisms of John took place.)

29 On the following day, John saw Jesus coming towards him and said, "Look, there is the lamb of God who will take away the
30 sin of the world! This is the man I meant when I said 'A man comes after me who is always in front of me, for he existed before
31 I was born!' It is true I have not known him, yet it was to make him known to the people of Israel that I came and baptised people with water."

32 Then John gave this testimony, "I have seen the Spirit come
33 down like a dove from Heaven and rest upon him. Indeed, it is true that I did not recognise him by myself, but he who sent me to baptise with water told me this: 'The one on whom you will see the Spirit coming down and resting is the man who baptises
34 with the Holy Spirit!' Now I have seen this happen and I declare publicly before you all that he is the Son of God!"

18

Men begin to follow Jesus

On the following day John was again standing with two of his 35
disciples. He looked straight at Jesus as he walked along and said, 36
"There is the lamb of God!" The two disciples heard what he 37
said and followed Jesus. Then Jesus turned round and when he 38
saw them following him, spoke to them. "What do you want?"
he said.

"Master, where are you staying?" they replied.

"Come and see," returned Jesus. 39

So they went and saw where he was staying and remained with
him the rest of that day. (It was then about four o'clock in the
afternoon.) One of the two men who had heard what John said 40
and had followed Jesus was Andrew, Simon Peter's brother. He 41
went straight off and found his own brother, Simon, and told
him, "We have found the Messiah!" (meaning, of course, Christ).
And he brought him to Jesus. 42

Jesus looked steadily at him and said, "You are Simon, the son
of John. From now on your name is Cephas" – (that is, Peter,
meaning "a rock").

The following day Jesus decided to go into Galilee. He found 43
Philip and said to him, "Follow me!" Philip was a man from 44
Bethsaida, the town that Andrew and Peter came from. Now 45
Philip found Nathanael and told him, "We have discovered the
man whom Moses wrote about in the Law and about whom the
Prophets wrote too. He is Jesus, the son of Joseph and comes from
Nazareth."

"Can anything good come out of Nazareth?" retorted 46
Nathanael.

"You come and see," replied Philip.

Jesus saw Nathanael coming towards him and remarked, "Now 47
here is a true man of Israel; there is no deceit in him!"

"How can you know me?" returned Nathanael. 48

"When you were underneath that fig-tree," replied Jesus,
"before Philip called you, I saw you."

At which Nathanael exclaimed, "Master, you are the Son of 49
God, you are the king of Israel!"

"Do you believe in me," replied Jesus, "because I said I had 50
seen you underneath that fig-tree? You are going to see something

51 greater than that! Believe me," he added, "I tell you all that you
will see Heaven wide open and God's angels ascending and descending around the Son of Man!"

CHAPTER II

The Son of God and a village wedding

1 Two days later there was a wedding in the Galilean village of
2 Cana. Jesus' mother was there and he and his disciples were
3 invited to the festivities. Then it happened that the supply of
wine gave out, and Jesus' mother told him, "They have no more
wine."

4 "Is that your concern, or mine?" replied Jesus. "My time has
not come yet."

5 So his mother said to the servants, "Mind you do whatever he
tells you."

6 In the room six very large stone water-jars stood on the floor
(actually for the Jewish ceremonial cleansing), each holding about
7 twenty gallons. Jesus gave instructions for these jars to be filled
8 with water, and the servants filled them to the brim. Then he
said to them, "Now draw some out and take it to the master of
9 ceremonies", which they did. When this man tasted the water,
which had now become wine, without knowing where it came
from (though naturally the servants who had drawn the water
10 knew), he called out to the bridegroom and said to him, "Everybody I know puts his good wine on first and then when men have
had plenty to drink, he brings out the poor stuff. But you have
11 kept back your good wine till now!" Jesus gave this, the first of
his signs, at Cana in Galilee. He demonstrated his power and his
disciples believed in him.

Jesus in the Temple

12 After this incident, Jesus, accompanied by his mother, his
brothers and his disciples, went down to Capernaum and stayed

there a few days. The Jewish Passover was approaching and Jesus   13
made the journey up to Jerusalem. In the Temple he discovered   14
cattle and sheep dealers and pigeon-sellers, as well as money-
changers sitting at their tables. So he made a rough whip out of   15
rope and drove the whole lot of them, sheep and cattle as well,
out of the Temple. He sent the coins of the money-changers
flying and turned their tables upside down. Then he said to the   16
pigeon-dealers, "Take those things out of here. Don't you dare
turn my Father's house into a market!" His disciples remembered   17
the scripture –

The zeal of thine house shall eat me up.

As a result of this, the Jews said to him, "What sign can you   18
give us to justify what you are doing?"

"Destroy this temple," Jesus retorted, "and I will rebuild it in   19
three days!"

To which the Jews replied, "This Temple took forty-six years
to build, and are you going to rebuild it in three days?"   20

He was, in fact, speaking about the temple of his own body,   21
and when he was raised from the dead the disciples remembered   22
what he had said to them and that made them believe both the
scripture and what Jesus had said.

While he was in Jerusalem at Passover-time, during the festivi-   23
ties many believed in him as they saw the signs that he gave. But   24
Jesus, on his side, did not trust himself to them – for he knew them
all. He did not need anyone to tell him what people were like: 25
he understood human nature.

CHAPTER III

Jesus and a religious leader

ONE night Nicodemus, a leading Jew and a Pharisee, came to see   1, 2
Jesus.

"Master," he began, "we realise that you are a teacher who has
come from God. Obviously no one could show the signs that
you show unless God were with him."

3   "Believe me," returned Jesus, "a man cannot even see the kingdom of God without being born again."

4   "And how can a man who's getting old possibly be born?" replied Nicodemus. "How can he go back into his mother's womb and be born a second time?"

5   "I assure you," said Jesus, "that unless a man is born from
6   water and from spirit he cannot enter the kingdom of God. Flesh
7   gives birth to flesh and spirit gives birth to spirit: you must not be
8   surprised that I told you that all of you must be born again. The wind blows where it likes, you can hear the sound of it but you have no idea where it comes from and where it goes. Nor can you tell how a man is born by the wind of the Spirit."

9   "How on earth can things like this happen?" replied Nicodemus.
10   "So you are a teacher of Israel," said Jesus, "and you do not
11   recognise such things? I assure you that we are talking about something we really know and we are witnessing to something we have actually observed, yet men like you will not accept our
12   evidence. Yet if I have spoken to you about things which happen on this earth and you will not believe me, what chance is there that you will believe me if I tell you about what happens in Heaven?
13   No one has ever been up to Heaven except the Son of Man who
14   came down from Heaven. The Son of Man must be lifted above the heads of men – as Moses lifted up that serpent in the desert –
15, 16 so that any man who believes in him may have eternal life. For God loved the world so much that he gave his only Son, so that everyone who believes in him should not be lost, but should have
17   eternal life. You must understand that God has not sent his Son into the world to pass sentence upon it, but to save it – through
18   him. Any man who believes in him is not judged at all. It is the one who will not believe who stands already condemned, because
19   he will not believe in the character of God's only Son. This *is* the judgement – that light has entered the world and men have
20   preferred darkness to light because their deeds are evil. Anybody who does wrong hates the light and keeps away from it, for fear
21   his deeds may be exposed. But anybody who is living by the truth will come to the light to make it plain that all he has done has been done through God."

Jesus and John again

After this Jesus went into the country of Judaea with his 22
disciples and stayed there with them while the work of baptism
was being carried on. John, too, was in Aenon near Salim, 23
baptising people because there was plenty of water in that district
and they were still coming to him for baptism. (John, of course, 24
had not yet been put in prison.)

This led to a question arising between John's disciples and one 25
of the Jews about the whole matter of being cleansed. They 26
approached John and said to him, "Master, look, the man who was
with you on the other side of the Jordan, the one you testified to,
is now baptising and everybody is coming to him!"

"A man can receive nothing at all," replied John, "unless it is 27
given him from Heaven. You yourselves can witness that I said, 28
'I am not Christ but I have been sent as his forerunner.' It is the 29
bridegroom who possesses the bride, yet the bridegroom's friend
who merely stands and listens to him can be overjoyed to hear
the bridegroom's voice. That is why my happiness is now complete. He must grow greater and greater and I less and less. 30

"The one who comes from above is naturally above everybody. 31
The one who arises from the earth belongs to the earth and speaks
from the earth. The one who comes from Heaven is above all
others and he bears witness to what he has seen and heard – yet 32
no one is accepting his testimony. Yet if a man does accept it, 33
he is acknowledging the fact that God is true. For the one whom 34
God sent speaks the authentic words of God – and there can
be no measuring of the Spirit given to *him*! The Father loves 35
the Son and has put everything into his hand. The man who 36
believes in the Son has eternal life. The man who refuses to
believe in the Son will not see life; he lives under the anger of
God."

CHAPTER IV

Jesus meets a Samaritan woman

1 Now, when the Lord found that the Pharisees had heard that "Jesus is making and baptising more disciples than John" –
2 although, in fact, it was not Jesus who did the baptising but his
3, 4 disciples – he left Judaea and went off again to Galilee, which
5 meant his passing through Samaria. There he came to a little town called Sychar, which is near the historic plot of land that Jacob
6 gave to his son, Joseph, and "Jacob's Spring" was there. Jesus, tired with the journey, sat down beside it, just as he was. The time
7 was about midday. Presently, a Samaritan woman arrived to draw some water.
8 "Please give me a drink," Jesus said to her, for his disciples had
9 gone away to the town to buy food. The Samaritan woman said to him, "How can you, a Jew, ask for a drink from me, a woman of Samaria?" (For Jews have no dealings with Samaritans.)
10 "If you knew what God can give," Jesus replied, "and if you knew who it is that said to you, 'Give me a drink', I think you would have asked him, and he would have given you living water!"
11 "Sir," said the woman, "you have nothing to draw water with
12 and this well is deep – where can you get your living water? Are you a greater man than our ancestor, Jacob, who gave us this well, and drank here himself with his family, and his cattle?"
13 Jesus said to her, "Everyone who drinks this water will be
14 thirsty again. But whoever drinks the water I will give him will never be thirsty again. For my gift will become a spring in the man himself, welling up into eternal life."
15 The woman said, "Sir, give me this water, so that I may stop being thirsty – and not have to come here to draw water any more!"
16 "Go and call your husband and then come back here," said Jesus to her.
17 "I haven't got a husband!" the woman answered.
"You are quite right in saying, 'I haven't got a husband',"

replied Jesus, "for you have had five husbands and the man you   *18*
have now is not your husband at all. Yes, you spoke the simple
truth when you said that."

"Sir," said the woman again, "I can see that you are a prophet!   *19*
Now our ancestors worshipped on this hill-side, but you Jews   *20*
say that Jerusalem is the place where men ought to worship —"

"Believe me," returned Jesus, "the time is coming when wor-   *21*
shipping the Father will not be a matter of 'on this hill-side' or
'in Jerusalem'. Nowadays you are worshipping with your eyes   *22*
shut. We Jews are worshipping with our eyes open, for the salvation of mankind is to come from our race. Yet the time is coming,   *23*
yes, and has already come, when true worshippers will worship the
Father in spirit and in reality. Indeed, the Father looks for men
who will worship him like that. God is Spirit, and those who   *24*
worship him can only worship in spirit and in reality."

"Of course I know that Messiah is coming," returned the   *25*
woman, "you know, the one who is called Christ. When he
comes he will make everything plain to us."

"I am Christ speaking to you now," said Jesus.   *26*

At this point his disciples arrived, and were very surprised to   *27*
find him talking to a woman, but none of them asked, "What do
you want?" or "What are you talking to her about?" So the   *28*
woman left her water-pot behind and went into the town and
began to say to the people, "Come out and see the man who   *29*
told me everything I've ever done! Can this be 'Christ'?" So they   *30*
left the town and started to come to Jesus.

Meanwhile the disciples were begging him, "Master, do eat   *31*
something."

To which Jesus replied, "I have food to eat that you know   *32*
nothing about."

This, of course, made the disciples ask each other, "Do you   *33*
think anyone has brought him any food?"

Jesus said to them, "My food is doing the will of him who sent   *34*
me and finishing the work he has given me. Don't you say, 'Four   *35*
months more and then comes the harvest'? But I tell you to open
your eyes and look at the fields – they are gleaming white, all
ready for the harvest! The reaper is already being rewarded and   *36*
getting in a harvest for eternal life, so that both sower and reaper
may be glad together. For in this harvest the old saying comes   *37*

25

38 true, 'One man sows and another reaps.' I have sent you to reap a harvest for which you never laboured; other men have worked hard and you have reaped the result of their labours."

39 Many of the Samaritans who came out of that town believed in him through the woman's testimony – "He told me everything
40 I've ever done." And when they arrived they begged him to stay
41 with them. He did stay there two days and far more believed in
42 him because of what he himself said. As they told the woman, "We don't believe any longer now because of what you said. We have heard him with our own ears. We know now that this must be the man who will save the world!"

Jesus, in Cana again, heals in response to faith

43 After the two days were over, Jesus left and went away to
44 Galilee. (For Jesus himself testified that a prophet enjoys no
45 honour in his own country.) And on his arrival the people received him with open arms. For they had seen all that he had done in Jerusalem during the festival, since they had themselves been
46 present. So Jesus came again to Cana in Galilee, the place where he had made the water into wine. At Capernaum there was an
47 official whose son was very ill. When he heard that Jesus had left Judaea and had arrived in Galilee, he went off to see him and begged him to come down and heal his son, who was by this time at the point of death.

48 Jesus said to him, "I suppose you will never believe unless you see signs and wonders!"

49 "Sir," returned the official, "please come down before my boy dies!"

50 "You can go home," returned Jesus, "your son is alive and well."

And the man believed what Jesus had said to him and went on his way.

51 On the journey back his servants met him with the report: "Your son is alive and well." So he asked them at what time he
52 had begun to recover, and they replied: "The fever left him
53 yesterday at one o'clock in the afternoon." Then the father knew that this must have happened at the very moment when Jesus had said to him, "Your son is alive and well." And he and his whole

household believed in Jesus. This, then, was the second sign that 54
Jesus gave on his return from Judaea to Galilee.

CHAPTER V

Jesus heals in Jerusalem

SOME time later came one of the Jewish feast-days and Jesus 1
went up to Jerusalem. There is in Jerusalem near the sheep-gate 2
a pool surrounded by five arches, which has the Hebrew name of
Bethzatha. Under these arches a great many sick people were in 3
the habit of lying; some of them were blind, some lame, and
some had withered limbs. (They used to wait there for the
"moving of the water", for at certain times an angel used to come 4
down into the pool and disturb the water, and then the first
person who stepped into the water after the disturbance would
be healed of whatever he was suffering from.) One particular 5
man had been there ill for thirty-eight years. When Jesus saw 6
him lying there on his back – knowing that he had been like
that for a long time, he said to him, "Do you want to get well
again?"

"Sir," replied the sick man, "I just haven't got anybody to put 7
me into the pool when the water is all stirred up. While I'm
trying to get there somebody else gets down into it first."

"Get up," said Jesus, "pick up your bed and walk!" 8

At once the man recovered, picked up his bed and walked. 9

This happened on a Sabbath day, which made the Jews keep 10
on telling the man who had been healed, "It's the Sabbath, you
know; it's not right for you to carry your bed."

"The man who made me well," he replied, "was the one who 11
told me, 'Pick up your bed and walk.'"

Then they asked him, "And who is the man who told you to 12
do that?"

But the one who had been healed had no idea who it was, for 13
Jesus had slipped away in the dense crowd. Later Jesus found him 14
in the Temple and said to him, "Look: you are a fit man now.
Do not sin again or something worse might happen to you!"

15 Then the man went off and informed the Jews that the one who
16 had made him well was Jesus. It was because Jesus did such things
17 on the Sabbath day that the Jews persecuted him. But Jesus'
answer to them was this, "My Father is still at work and therefore
I work as well."
18 This remark made the Jews all the more determined to kill
him, because not only did he break the Sabbath but he referred
to God as his own Father, so putting himself on equal terms
with God.

Jesus makes his tremendous claim

19 Jesus said to them, "I assure you that the Son can do nothing
of his own accord, but only what he sees the Father doing. What
20 the Son does is always modelled on what the Father does, for the
Father loves the Son and shows him everything that he does himself. Yes, and he will show him even greater things than these to
21 fill you with wonder. For just as the Father raises the dead and
makes them live, so does the Son give life to any man he chooses.
22 The Father is no man's judge: he has put judgement entirely into
23 the Son's hands, so that all men may honour the Son equally with
the Father. The man who does not honour the Son does not
24 honour the Father who sent him. I solemnly assure you that the
man who hears what I have to say and believes in the one who has
sent me has eternal life. He does not have to face judgement; he
25 has already passed from death into life. Yes, I assure you that a
time is coming, in fact has already come, when the dead will hear
the voice of the Son of God and when they have heard it they will
26 live! For just as the Father has life in himself, so by the Father's
27 gift, the Son also has life in himself. And he has given him author-
28 ity to judge because he is Son of Man. No, do not be surprised
– the time is coming when all those who are dead and buried
29 will hear his voice and out they will come – those who have done
right will rise again to life, but those who have done wrong will
rise to face judgement!
30 "By myself I can do nothing. As I hear, I judge, and my judgement is true because I do not live to please myself but to do the
31 will of the Father who sent me. You may say that I am bearing
witness about myself, that therefore what I say about myself has

no value, but I would remind you that there is one who witnesses   *32*
about me and I know that his witness about me is absolutely true.
You sent to John, and he testified to the truth. Not that it is   *33, 34*
man's testimony that I accept – I only tell you this to help you
to be saved. John certainly was a lamp that burned and shone,   *35*
and for a time you were willing to enjoy the light that he gave.   *36*
But I have a higher testimony than John's. The work that the
Father gave me to complete, yes, these very actions which I
do are my witness that the Father has sent me. This is how the   *37*
Father who has sent me has given his own personal testimony to
me.

"Now you have never at any time heard what he says or seen
what he is like. Nor do you really believe his word in your hearts,   *38*
for you refuse to believe the man whom he has sent. You pore   *39*
over the scriptures, for you imagine that you will find eternal life
in them. And all the time they give their testimony to me! But you   *40*
are not willing to come to me to have real life! Men's approval   *41*
or disapproval means nothing to me, but I can tell that you have   *42*
none of the love of God in your hearts. I have come in the name   *43*
of my Father and you will not accept me. Yet if another man
comes simply in his own name, you will accept him. How on   *44*
earth can you believe while you are for ever looking for each
other's approval and not for the glory that comes from the one
God? There is no need for you to think that I have come to accuse   *45*
you before the Father. You already have an accuser – Moses, in
whom you put all your confidence! For if you really believed   *46*
Moses, you would be bound to believe me; for it was about me
that he wrote. But if you do not believe what he wrote, how can   *47*
you believe what I say?"

CHAPTER VI

Jesus shows his power over material things

AFTER this, Jesus crossed the Lake of Galilee (or Tiberias), and   *1, 2*
a great crowd followed him because they had seen the signs which

3 he gave in his dealings with the sick. But Jesus went up the hill-
4 side and sat down there with his disciples. The Passover, the
5 Jewish festival, was near. So Jesus, raising his eyes and seeing a
great crowd on their way towards him, said to Philip, "Where
6 can we buy food for these people to eat?" (He said this to test
Philip, for he himself knew what he was going to do.)
7 "Ten pounds' worth of bread would not be enough for them,"
Philip replied, "even if they had only a little each."
8 Then Andrew, Simon Peter's brother, another disciple, put in,
9 "There is a boy here who has five small barley loaves and a couple
of fish, but what's the good of that for such a crowd?"
10 Then Jesus said, "Get the people to sit down."
There was plenty of grass there, and the men, some five
11 thousand of them, sat down. Then Jesus took the loaves, gave
thanks for them and distributed them to the people sitting on the
grass, and he distributed the fish in the same way, giving them as
12 much as they wanted. When they had eaten enough, Jesus said
to his disciples, "Collect the pieces that are left over so that
nothing is wasted."
13 So they did as he suggested and filled twelve baskets with the
broken pieces of the five barley loaves, which were left over after
14 the people had eaten! When the men saw this sign of Jesus'
power, they kept saying, "This certainly is the Prophet who was
to come into the world!"
15 Then Jesus, realising that they were going to carry him off and
make him their king, retired once more to the hill-side quite alone.
16, 17 In the evening, his disciples went down to the lake, embarked
on the boat and made their way across the lake to Capernaum.
Darkness had already fallen and Jesus had not returned to them.
18, 19 A strong wind sprang up and the water grew very rough. When
they had rowed about three or four miles, they saw Jesus walking
on the water and coming towards the boat, and they were terrified.
20 But he spoke to them, "Don't be afraid: it is I myself."
21 So they gladly took him aboard, and at once the boat reached
the shore they were making for.

Jesus teaches about the true bread

22 The following day, the crowd, who had remained on the other

side of the lake, noticed that only the one boat had been there, and that Jesus had not embarked on it with his disciples, but that they had in fact gone off by themselves. Some other small boats from 23 Tiberias had landed quite near the place where they had eaten the food and the Lord had given thanks. When the crowd realised 24 that neither Jesus nor the disciples were there any longer, they themselves got into the boats and went off to Capernaum to look for Jesus. When they had found him on the other side of the lake, 25 they said to him, "Master, when did you come here?"

"Believe me," replied Jesus, "you are looking for me now not 26 because you saw my signs but because you ate that food and had all you wanted. You should not work for the food which does 27 not last but for the food which lasts on into eternal life. This is the food the Son of Man will give you, and he is the one who bears the stamp of God the Father."

This made them ask him, "What must we do to carry out the 28 work of God?"

"The work of God for you," replied Jesus, "is to believe in the 29 one whom he has sent to you."

Then they asked him, "Then what sign can you give us that 30 will make us believe in you? What work are you doing? Our 31 forefathers ate manna in the desert just as the scripture says,

He gave them bread out of Heaven to eat."

To which Jesus replied, "Yes, but what matters is not that 32 Moses *gave you* bread from Heaven but that my Father is *giving you* the true bread from Heaven. For the bread of God which 33 comes down from Heaven gives life to the world."

This made them say to him, "Lord, please give us this bread, 34 always!"

Then Jesus said to them, "I myself am the bread of life. The 35 man who comes to me will never be hungry and the man who believes in me will never again be thirsty. Yet I have told you that 36 you have seen me and do not believe. Everything that my Father 37 gives me will come to me and I will never refuse anyone who comes to me. For I have come down from Heaven, not to do what 38 I want, but to do the will of him who sent me. The will of him who 39 sent me is that I should not lose anything of what he has given me, but should raise it up when the last day comes. And this is 40 the will of the one who sent me, that everyone who sees the Son

and trusts him should have eternal life, and I will raise him up
when the last day comes."

41 At this, the Jews began grumbling at him because he said, "I am
42 the bread which came down from Heaven", remarking "Is not
this Jesus, the son of Joseph, whose parents we know? How can
he say that 'I have come down from Heaven'?"

43 So Jesus answered them, "Do not grumble among yourselves.
44 Nobody comes to me unless he is drawn to me by the Father who
45 sent me, and I will raise him up when the last day comes. In the
Prophets it is written –

'And they shall all be taught of God,'
and this means that everybody who has heard the Father's voice
46 and learned from him will come to me. Not that anyone has ever
seen the Father except the one who comes from God – he has seen
47 the Father. I assure you that the man who trusts in him has eternal
48, 49 life already. I myself am the bread of life. Your forefathers ate
50 manna in the desert, *and they died*. This is bread that comes down
51 from Heaven, so that a man may eat it and not die. I myself
am the living bread which came down from Heaven, and if
anyone eats this bread he will live for ever. The bread which I
will give is my body and I shall give it for the life of the world."

52 This led to a fierce argument among the Jews, some of them
saying, "How can this man give us his body to eat?"

53 So Jesus said to them, "Unless you do eat the body of the Son
54 of Man and drink his blood, you are not really living at all. The
man who eats my flesh and drinks my blood has eternal life and
55 I will raise him up when the last day comes. For my body is real
56 food and my blood is real drink. The man who eats my body and
57 drinks my blood shares my life and I share his. Just as the living
Father sent me and I am alive because of the Father, so the man
58 who lives on me will live because of me. *This* is the bread which
came down from Heaven! It is not like the manna which your
forefathers used to eat, *and died*. The man who eats this bread will
live for ever."

59 Jesus said all these things while teaching in the synagogue at
60 Capernaum. Many of his disciples heard him say these things, and
commented, "This is hard teaching indeed; who could accept
that?"

61 Then Jesus, knowing intuitively that his disciples were com-

32

plaining about what he had just said, went on, "Is this too much
for you? Then what would happen if you were to see the Son of   62
Man going up to the place where he was before? It is the Spirit   63
which gives life. The flesh will not help you. The things which I
have told you are spiritual and are life. But some of you will not   64
believe me."

For Jesus knew from the beginning which of his followers did
not trust him and who was the man who would betray him. Then   65
he added, "This is why I said to you, 'No one can come to me
unless my Father puts it into his heart to come.'"

As a consequence of this, many of his disciples withdrew and   66
no longer followed him. So Jesus said to the twelve, "And are   67
you too wanting to go away?"

"Lord," answered Simon Peter, "who else should we go to?   68
Your words have the ring of eternal life! And we believe and are   69
convinced that you are the holy one of God."

Jesus replied, "Did I not choose you twelve – and one of you   70
has the devil in his heart?"

He was speaking of Judas, the son of Simon Iscariot, one of   71
the twelve, who was planning to betray him.

CHAPTER VII

Jesus delays his arrival at the festival

AFTER this, Jesus moved about in Galilee but decided not to do   1
so in Judaea since the Jews were planning to take his life. A Jewish   2
festival, "The feast of the tabernacles", was approaching and his   3
brothers said to him, "You ought to leave here and go to Judaea   4
so that your disciples can see what you are doing, for nobody
works in secret if he wants to be known publicly. If you are
going to do things like this, let the world see what you are doing."
For not even his brothers had any faith in him. Jesus replied by   5, 6
saying, "It is not yet the right time for me, but any time is right
for you. You see, it is impossible for you to arouse the world's   7
hatred, but I provoke hatred because I show the world how evil

C   33

8 its deeds really are. No, you go up to the festival; I shall not go
9 up now, for it is not yet time for me to go." And after these
remarks he remained where he was in Galilee.

10 Later, after his brothers had gone up to the festival, he went
up himself, not openly but as though he did not want to be seen.
11 Consequently, the Jews kept looking for him at the festival and
12 asking "Where is that man?" And there was an undercurrent of
discussion about him among the crowds. Some would say, "He
is a good man", others maintained that he was not, but that he
13 was "misleading the people". Nobody, however, spoke openly
about him for fear of the Jews.

Jesus openly declares his authority

14 But at the very height of the festival, Jesus went up to the
15 Temple and began teaching. The Jews were amazed and remarked,
"How does this man know all this – he has never been taught?"
16 Jesus replied to them, "My teaching is not really mine but
17 comes from the one who sent me. If anyone wants to do God's
will, he will know whether my teaching is from God or whether
18 I merely speak on my own authority. A man who speaks on his
own authority has an eye for his own reputation. But the man who
is considering the glory of God who sent him is a true man.
There can be no dishonesty about him.

19 "Did not Moses give you the Law? Yet not a single one of you
obeys the Law. Why are you trying to kill me?"

20 The crowd answered, "You must be mad! Who is trying to
kill you?"

21 Jesus answered them, "I have done one thing and you are all
22 amazed at it. Moses gave you circumcision (not that it came from
Moses originally but from your forefathers), and you will cir-
23 cumcise a man even on the Sabbath. If a man receives the cutting
of circumcision on the Sabbath to avoid breaking the Law of
Moses, why should you be angry with me because I have made a
24 man's body perfectly whole on the Sabbath? You must not judge
by the appearance of things but by the reality!"

25 Some of the people of Jerusalem, hearing him talk like this,
26 were saying, "Isn't this the man whom they are trying to kill? It's
amazing – he talks quite openly and they haven't a word to say

34

to him. Surely our rulers haven't decided that this really is Christ!
But then, we know this man and where he comes from – when   27
Christ comes, no one will know where he comes from."

Jesus makes more unique claims

Then Jesus, in the middle of his teaching, called out in the   28
Temple, "So you know me and know where I have come from?
But I have not come of my own accord; I am sent by one who is
true and you do not know him! I do know him, because I come   29
from him and he has sent me here."

Then they attempted to arrest him, but actually no one laid   30
a finger on him because the right moment had not yet come. Many   31
of the crowd believed in him and kept on saying, "When Christ
comes, is he going to show greater signs than this man?"

The Pharisees heard the crowd whispering these things about   32
him, and they and the chief priests sent officers to arrest him.
Then Jesus said, "I shall be with you only a little while longer and   33
then I am going to him who sent me. You will look for me then   34
but you will never find me. You cannot come where I shall be."

This made the Jews say to each other, "Where is he going to   35
hide himself so that we cannot find him? Surely he's not going
to our refugees among the Greeks to teach Greeks? What does he   36
mean when he says, 'You will look for me and you will never
find me' and 'You cannot come where I shall be'?"

Then, on the last day, the climax of the festival, Jesus stood up
and cried out, "If any man is thirsty, he can come to me and drink!   37
The man who believes in me, as the scripture said, will have   38
rivers of living water flowing from his inmost heart." (Here he   39
was speaking about the Spirit which those who believe in him
would receive. The Holy Spirit had not yet been given because
Jesus had not yet been glorified.) When they heard these words,   40
some of the people were saying, "This really is the Prophet."
Others said, "This is Christ!" But some said, "And does Christ   41
come from Galilee? Don't the scriptures say that Christ will be   42
descended from David, and will come from Bethlehem, the
village where David lived?"

So the people were in two minds about him – some of them   43, 44
wanted to arrest him, but so far no one laid hands on him.

45   Then the officers returned to the Pharisees and chief priests, who said to them, "Why haven't you brought him?"

46   "No man ever spoke like that!" they replied.

47   "Has he pulled the wool over your eyes, too?" retorted the
48   Pharisees. "Have any of the authorities or any of the Pharisees
49   believed in him? But this crowd, who know nothing about the Law, is damned anyway!"

50   One of their number, Nicodemus (the one who had previously
51   been to see Jesus), remarked to them, "But surely our Law does not condemn the accused without hearing what he has to say, and finding out what he has done?"

52   "Are you a Galilean, too?" they answered him. "Look where you will – you won't find that any prophet comes out of Galilee!"

53   So they broke up their meeting and went home, while Jesus
VIII 1 went off to the Mount of Olives.*

CHAPTER VIII

Jesus deflates the rigorists

2   EARLY next morning he returned to the Temple and the entire crowd came to him. So he sat down and began to teach them.
3   But the scribes and Pharisees brought in to him a woman who had
4   been caught in adultery. They made her stand in front, and then said to him, "Now, master, this woman has been caught in
5   adultery, in the very act. According to the Law, Moses commanded us to stone such women to death. Now, what do you say about her?"

6   They said this to test him, so that they might have some good grounds for an accusation. But Jesus stooped down and began to
7   write with his finger in the dust on the ground. But as they persisted in their questioning, he straightened himself up and said

* vii. 53 to 8–11—The Woman taken in Adultery.

This passage has no place in the oldest manuscripts of John, and is considered by most scholars to be an interpolation from some [other source. Almost all scholars would agree that, although the story is out of place here, it is part of a genuine apostolic tradition.

to them, "Let the one among you who has never sinned throw
the first stone at her." Then he stooped down again and con-   8
tinued writing with his finger on the ground. And when they   9
heard what he said, they were convicted by their own consciences
and went out, one by one, beginning with the eldest until they
had all gone.

Jesus was left alone, with the woman still standing where they
had put her. So he stood up and said to her, "Where are they all   10
– did no one condemn you?"

And she said, "No one, sir."   11

"Neither do I condemn you," said Jesus to her. "Go home and
do not sin again."

Jesus' bold claims – about himself – and his Father

Later, Jesus spoke to the people again and said, "I am the light   12
of the world. The man who follows me will never walk in the
dark but will live his life in the light."

This made the Pharisees say to him, "You are testifying to   13
yourself – your evidence is not valid."

Jesus answered, "Even if I am testifying to myself, my evidence   14
is valid, for I know where I have come from and I know where
I am going. But as for you, you have no idea where I come from
or where I am going. You are judging by human standards, but   15
I am not judging anyone. Yet if I should judge, my decision   16
would be just, for I am not alone – the Father who sent me is with
me. In your Law, it is stated that the witness of two persons is   17
valid. I am one testifying to myself and the second witness to me   18
is the Father who sent me."

"And where is this father of yours?" they replied.   19

"You do not know my Father," returned Jesus, "any more than
you know me: if you had known me, you would have known
him."

Jesus made these statements while he was teaching in the   20
Temple treasury. Yet no one arrested him, for his time had not
yet come.

Later, Jesus spoke to them again and said, "I am going away   21
and you will try to find me, but you will die in your sins. You
cannot come where I am going."

22   This made the Jews say, "Is he going to kill himself, then? Is *that* why he says, 'You cannot come where I am going'?"

23   "The difference between us," Jesus said to them, "is that you come from below and I am from above. You belong to this world
24 but I do not. That is why I told you you will die in your sins. For unless you believe that I am who I am, you will die in your sins."

25   Then they said, "*Who are you?*"

   "I am what I have told you I was from the beginning," replied
26 Jesus. "There is much in you that I could speak about and condemn. But he who sent me is true and I am only speaking to this world what I myself have heard from him."

27   They did not realise that he was talking to them about the
28 Father. So Jesus resumed, "When you have lifted up the Son of Man, then you will realise that I am who I say I am, and that I do nothing on my own authority but speak simply as my Father
29 has taught me. The one who sent me is with me now: the Father
30 has never left me alone for I always do what pleases him." And even while he said these words, many people believed in him.

Jesus speaks of personal freedom

31   So Jesus said to the Jews who believed in him, "If you are
32 faithful to what I have said, you are truly my disciples. And you will know the truth and the truth will set you free!"

33   "But we are descendants of Abraham," they replied, "and we have never in our lives been any man's slaves. How can you say to us, 'You will be set free'?"

34   Jesus returned, "Believe me when I tell you that every man who
35 commits sin is a slave. For a slave is no permanent part of a house-
36 hold, but a son is. If the Son, then, sets you free, you are really
37 free! I know that you are descended from Abraham, but some of you are looking for a way to kill me because you can't bear my
38 words. I am telling you what I have seen in the presence of my Father, and you are doing what you have seen in the presence of your father."

39   "Our father is Abraham!" they retorted.

   "If you were the children of Abraham, you would do the sort
40 of things Abraham did. But in fact, at this moment, you are looking for a way to kill me, simply because I am a man who has

told you the truth that I have heard from God. Abraham would never have done that. No, you are doing your father's work." 41

"We are not illegitimate!" they retorted. "We have one Father – God."

"If God were really your Father," replied Jesus, "you would 42 have loved me. For I came from God; and I am here. I did not come of my own accord – he sent me, and I am here. Why do 43 you not understand my words? It is because you cannot hear what I am really saying. Your father is the devil, and what you 44 are wanting to do is what your father longs to do. He always was a murderer, and has never dealt with the truth, since the truth will have nothing to do with him. Whenever he tells a lie, he speaks in character, for he is a liar and the father of lies. And it 45 is because I speak the truth that you will not believe me. Which 46 of you can prove me guilty of sin? If I am speaking the truth, why is it that you do not believe me? The man who is born of 47 God can hear the words of God and the reason why you cannot hear the words of God is simply this, that you are not the sons of God."

"How right we are," retorted the Jews, "in calling you a 48 Samaritan, and mad at that!"

"No," replied Jesus, "I am not mad. I am honouring my 49 Father and you are trying to dishonour me. But I am not con- 50 cerned with my own glory: there is one whose concern it is, and he is the true judge. Believe me when I tell you that if anybody 51 accepts my words, he will never see death at all."

"Now we know that you're mad," replied the Jews. "Why, 52 Abraham died and the prophets, too, and yet you say, 'If a man accepts my words, he will never experience death!' Are you 53 greater than our father, Abraham? He died, and so did the prophets – who are you making yourself out to be?"

"If I were trying to glorify myself," returned Jesus, "such glory 54 would be worthless. But it is my Father who glorifies me, the very one whom you say is your God – though you have never 55 known him. But I know him, and if I said I did not know him, I should be as much a liar as you are! But I do know him and I am faithful to what he says. As for your father, Abraham, his great 56 joy was that he would see my coming. Now he has seen it and he is overjoyed."

57 "Look," said the Jews to him, "you are not fifty yet – and has Abraham seen you?"

58 "I tell you in solemn truth," returned Jesus, "before there was an Abraham, I AM!"

59 At this, they picked up stones to hurl at him, but Jesus disappeared and made his way out of the Temple.

CHAPTER IX

Jesus and blindness, physical and spiritual

1 LATER, as Jesus walked along he saw a man who had been blind from birth.

2 "Master, whose sin caused this man's blindness," asked the disciples, "his own or his parents'?"

3 "He was not born blind because of his own sin or that of his parents," returned Jesus, "but to show the power of God at work

4 in him. We must carry on the work of him who sent me while

5 the daylight lasts. Night is coming, when no one can work. I am the world's light as long as I am in it."

6 Having said this, he spat on the ground and made a sort of clay

7 with the saliva. This he applied to the man's eyes and said, "Go and wash in the pool of Siloam." (Siloam means "one who has been sent".) So the man went off and washed and came home with his sight restored.

8 His neighbours and the people who had often seen him before as a beggar remarked, "Isn't this the man who used to sit and beg?"

9 "Yes, that's the one," said some.

Others said, "No, but he's very like him."

But he himself said, "I'm the man all right!"

10 "Then how was your blindness cured?" they asked.

11 "The man called Jesus made some clay and smeared it on my eyes," he replied, "and then he said, 'Go to Siloam and wash.' So off I went and washed – and that's how I got my sight!"

12 "Where is he now?" they asked.

"I don't know," he returned.

So they brought the man who had once been blind before the 13
Pharisees. (It should be noted that Jesus made the clay and 14
restored his sight on a Sabbath day.) The Pharisees asked the 15
question all over again as to how he had become able to see.

"He put clay on my eyes; I washed it off; now I can see –
that's all," he replied.

Some of the Pharisees commented, "This man cannot be from 16
God since he does not observe the Sabbath."

"But how can a sinner give such wonderful signs as these?"
others demurred. And they were in two minds about him.
Finally, they asked the blind man again, "And what do *you* say 17
about him? You're the one whose sight was restored."

"I believe he is a prophet," he replied.

The Jews did not really believe that the man had been blind and 18
then had become able to see, until they had summoned his parents
and asked them, "Is this your son who you say was born blind? 19
How does it happen that he can now see?"

"We know that this is our son, and we know that he was born 20
blind," returned his parents, "but how he can see now, or who 21
made him able to see, we have no idea. Why don't you ask him?
He is a grown-up man; he can speak for himself."

His parents said this because they were afraid of the Jews who 22
had already agreed that anybody who admitted that Christ
had done this thing should be excommunicated. It was this 23
fear which made his parents say, "Ask him, he is a grown-up
man."

So, once again they summoned the man who had been born 24
blind and said to him, "You should give God the glory for what
has happened to you. We know that this man is a sinner."

"Whether he is a sinner or not, I couldn't tell, but one thing 25
I am sure of," the man replied, "I used to be blind, now I can
see!"

"But what did he *do* to you – how did he make you see?" they 26
continued.

"I've told you before," he replied. "Weren't you listening? 27
Why do you want to hear it all over again? Are you wanting to
be his disciples too?"

At this, they turned on him furiously. 28

"You're the one who is his disciple! We are disciples of Moses.

29 We know that God spoke to Moses, but as for this man, we don't even know where he came from."

30 "Now here's the extraordinary thing," he retorted, "you don't know where he came from and yet he gave me the gift of sight.

31 Everybody knows that God does not listen to sinners. It is the man who has a proper respect for God and does what God wants

32 him to do – he's the one God listens to. Why, since the world began, nobody's ever heard of a man who was born blind being

33 given his sight. If this man did not come from God, he couldn't do such a thing!"

34 "You misbegotten wretch!" they flung back at him. "Are you trying to teach *us*?" And they threw him out.

35 Jesus heard that they had expelled him and when he had found him, he said, "Do you believe in the Son of Man?"

36 "And who is he, sir?" the man replied. "Tell me, so that I can believe in him."

37 "You have seen him," replied Jesus. "It is the one who is talking to you now."

38 "Lord, I do believe," he said, and worshipped him.

39 Then Jesus said, "My coming into this world is itself a judgement – those who cannot see have their eyes opened and those who think they can see become blind."

40 Some of the Pharisees near him overheard this and said, "So we're blind, too, are we?"

41 "If you were blind," returned Jesus, "nobody could blame you, but, as you insist 'We can see', your guilt remains."

CHAPTER X

Jesus declares himself the true shepherd of men

1 THEN Jesus said, "Believe me when I tell you that anyone who does not enter the sheepfold through the door, but climbs in by

2 some other way, is a thief and a rogue. It is the shepherd of the

3 flock who goes in by the door. It is to him the door-keeper opens the door and it is his voice that the sheep recognise. He calls his

own sheep by name and leads them out of the fold, and when he 4
has driven all his own flock outside, he goes in front of them himself, and the sheep follow him because they know his voice. They 5
will never follow a stranger – indeed, they will run away from
him, for they do not recognise strange voices."

Jesus gave them this illustration but they did not grasp the 6
point of what he was saying to them. So Jesus said to them once 7
more, "I do assure you that I myself am the door for the sheep.
All who have gone before me are like thieves and rogues, but the 8
sheep did not listen to them. I am the door. If a man goes in 9
through me, he will be safe and sound; he can come in and out
and find his food. The thief comes with the sole intention of steal- 10
ing and killing and destroying, but I came to bring them life,
and far more life than before. I am the good shepherd. The good 11
shepherd will give his life for the sake of his sheep. But the hired 12
man, who is not the shepherd, and does not own the sheep, will
see the wolf coming, desert the sheep and run away. And the wolf
will attack the flock and send them flying. The hired man runs 13
away because he is only a hired man and has no interest in the
sheep. I am the good shepherd, and I know those that are 14
mine and my sheep know me, just as the Father knows me and 15
I know the Father. And I am giving my life for the sake of the
sheep.

"And I have other sheep who do not belong to this fold. I 16
must lead these also, and they will hear my voice. So there will
be one flock and one shepherd. This is the reason why the Father 17
loves me – that I lay down my life, and I lay it down to take it
up again! No one is taking it from me, but I lay it down of my 18
own free will. I have the power to lay it down and I have the
power to take it up again. This is an order that I have received
from my Father."

Jesus plainly declares who he is

Once again, the Jews were in two minds about him because of 19
these words, many of them remarking, "The devil's in him and 20
he's insane. Why do you listen to him?"

But others were saying, "This is not the sort of thing a devil- 21
possessed man would say! Can a devil make a blind man see?"

22   Then came the dedication festival at Jerusalem. It was winter-
23   time and Jesus was walking about inside the Temple in Solomon's
24   cloisters. So the Jews closed in on him and said, "How much
longer are you going to keep us in suspense? If you really are
Christ, tell us so straight out!"

25   "I have told you," replied Jesus, "and you do not believe it.
What I have done in my Father's name is sufficient to prove my
26, 27   claim, but you do not believe because you are not my sheep. My
sheep recognise my voice, and I know who they are. They follow
28   me and I give them eternal life. They will never die and no one
29   can snatch them out of my hand. My Father, who has given them
to me, is greater than all. And no one can tear anything out of
30   the Father's hand. I and the Father are One."

31   Again the Jews reached for stones to stone him to death, but
32   Jesus answered them, "I have shown you many good things from
the Father – for which of these do you intend to stone me?"

33   "We're not going to stone you for any good things," replied
the Jews, "but for blasphemy: because you, who are only a man,
are making yourself out to be God."

34   "Is it not written in your own Law," replied Jesus, "'I have
35   said ye are gods'? And if he called those men 'gods' to whom the
36   word of God came (and the scripture cannot be broken), can you
say to the one whom the Father has consecrated and sent into the
world, 'You are blaspheming' because I said, 'I am the Son of
37   God'? If I fail to do what my Father does, then do not believe
38   me. But if I do, even though you have no faith in me personally,
then believe in the things that I do. Then you may come to know
and realise that the Father is in me and I am in the Father."

39   And again they tried to arrest him, but he moved out of their
reach.

40   Then Jesus went off again across the Jordan to the place where
41   John had first baptised and there he stayed. A great many people
came to him, and said, "John never gave us any sign but all that
he said about this man was true."

42   And in that place many believed in him.

CHAPTER XI

Jesus shows his power over death

NOW there was a man by the name of Lazarus who became   1
seriously ill. He lived in Bethany, the village where Mary and her
sister Martha lived. (Lazarus was the brother of the Mary who   2
poured perfume upon the Lord and wiped his feet with her hair.)
So the sisters sent word to Jesus: "Lord, your friend is very ill."   3
When Jesus received the message, he said, "This illness is not   4
meant to end in death; it is going to bring glory to God – for it
will show the glory of the Son of God."

Now Jesus loved Martha and her sister and Lazarus. So when   5, 6
he heard of Lazarus' illness he stayed where he was two days
longer. Only then did he say to the disciples, "Let us go back into   7
Judaea."

"Master!" returned the disciples, "only a few days ago, the   8
Jews were trying to stone you to death – are you going there
again?"

"There are twelve hours of daylight every day, are there not?"   9
replied Jesus. "If a man walks in the daytime, he does not stumble,
for he has the daylight to see by. But if he walks at night he   10
stumbles, because he cannot see where he is going."

Jesus spoke these words; then after a pause he said to them,   11
"Our friend Lazarus has fallen asleep, but I am going to wake
him up."

At this, his disciples said, "Lord, if he has fallen asleep, he will   12
be all right."

Actually Jesus had spoken about his death, but they thought   13
that he was speaking about falling into natural sleep. This made   14
Jesus tell them quite plainly, "Lazarus has died, and I am glad   15
that I was not there – for your sakes, that you may learn to
believe. And now, let us go to him."

Thomas (known as the twin) then said to his fellow-disciples,   16
"Come on, then, let us all go and die with him!"

When Jesus arrived, he found that Lazarus had already been in   17
the grave four days. Now Bethany is quite near Jerusalem, rather   18

45

19 less than two miles away, and a good many of the Jews had come
out to see Martha and Mary to offer them sympathy over their
20 brother's death. When Martha heard that Jesus was on his way,
she went out and met him, while Mary stayed in the house.

21 "If only you had been here, Lord," said Martha, "my brother
22 would never have died. And I know that, even now, God will
give you whatever you ask from him."

23 "Your brother will rise again," Jesus replied to her.

24 "I know," said Martha, "that he will rise again in the resurrection at the last day."

25 "I myself am the resurrection and the life," Jesus told her.
26 "The man who believes in me will live even though he dies, and
anyone who is alive and believes in me will never die at all. Can
you believe that?"

27 "Yes, Lord," replied Martha. "I do believe that you are Christ,
28 the Son of God, the one who was to come into the world." Saying this she went away and called Mary her sister, whispering,
29 "The master's here and is asking for you." When Mary heard this
30 she sprang to her feet and went to him. Now Jesus had not yet
arrived at the village itself, but was still where Martha had met
31 him. So when the Jews who had been condoling with Mary in
the house saw her get up quickly and go out, they followed her,
imagining that she was going to the grave to weep there.

32 When Mary met Jesus, she looked at him, and then fell down
at his feet. "If only you had been here, Lord," she said, "my
brother would never have died."

33 When Jesus saw Mary weep and noticed the tears of the Jews
who came with her, he was deeply moved and visibly distressed.

34 "Where have you put him?" he asked.

35 "Lord, come and see," they replied, and at this Jesus himself
wept.

36, 37 "Look how much he loved him!" remarked the Jews, though
some of them asked, "Could he not have kept this man from
dying if he could open that blind man's eyes?"

38 Jesus was again deeply moved at these words, and went on to
the grave. It was a cave, and a stone lay in front of it.

39 "Take away the stone," said Jesus.
"But Lord," said Martha, the dead man's sister, "he has been
dead four days. By this time he will be decaying. . . ."

"Did I not tell you," replied Jesus, "that if you believed, you 40
would see the wonder of what God can do?"

Then they took the stone away and Jesus raised his eyes and 41
said, "Father, I thank you that you have heard me. I know that 42
you always hear me, but I have said this for the sake of these
people standing here so that they may believe that you have
sent me."

And when he had said this, he called out in a loud voice, 43
"Lazarus, come out!"

And the dead man came out, his hands and feet bound with 44
grave-clothes and his face muffled with a handkerchief.

"Now unbind him," Jesus told them, "and let him go home."

Jesus' miracle leads to deadly hostility

After this many of the Jews who had accompanied Mary and 45
observed what Jesus did, believed in him. But some of them went 46
off to the Pharisees and told them what Jesus had done. Conse- 47
quently, the Pharisees and chief priests summoned the council
and said, "What can we do? This man obviously shows many
remarkable signs. If we let him go on doing this sort of thing we 48
shall have everybody believing in him. Then we shall have the
Romans coming and that will be the end of our holy place and
our very existence as a nation!"

But one of them, Caiaphas, who was High Priest that year, 49
addressed the meeting: "You plainly don't understand what is
involved here. You do not realise that it would be a good thing 50
for us if one man should die for the sake of the people – instead of
the whole nation being destroyed." (He did not make this remark 51
on his own initiative but, since he was High Priest that year, he
was in fact inspired to say that Jesus was going to die for the
nation's sake – and in fact not for that nation only, but to bring 52
together into one family all the children of God scattered throughout the world.) From that day then, they planned to kill him. As 53, 54
a consequence Jesus made no further public appearance among the
Jews but went away to the countryside on the edge of the desert,
and stayed with his disciples in a town called Ephraim. The Jewish 55
Passover was approaching and many people went up from the
country to Jerusalem before the actual Passover, to go through a

56 ceremonial cleansing. They were looking for Jesus there and kept saying to one another as they stood in the Temple, "What do you think? Surely he won't come to the festival?"

57 It should be understood that the chief priests and the Pharisees had issued an order that anyone who knew of Jesus' whereabouts should tell them, so that they could arrest him.

CHAPTER XII

An act of love as the end approaches

1 Six days before the Passover, Jesus came to Bethany, the village
2 of Lazarus whom he had raised from the dead. They gave a supper for him there, and Martha waited on the party while
3 Lazarus took his place at table with Jesus. Then Mary took a whole pound of very expensive perfume and anointed Jesus' feet and then wiped them with her hair. The entire house was filled with
4 the fragrance of the perfume. But one of his disciples, Judas Iscariot (the man who was going to betray Jesus), burst out,
5 "Why on earth wasn't this perfume sold? It's worth thirty pounds, which could have been given to the poor!"
6 He said this, not because he cared about the poor, but because he was dishonest, and when he was in charge of the purse used to help himself from the contents.
7 But Jesus replied to this outburst, "Let her alone, let her keep
8 this for the day of my burial. You have the poor with you always – you will not always have me!"
9 The large crowd of Jews discovered that he was there and came to the scene – not only because of Jesus but to catch sight of
10 Lazarus, the man whom he had raised from the dead. Then the
11 chief priests planned to kill Lazarus as well, because he was the reason for many of the Jews' going away and putting their faith in Jesus.

Jesus experiences a temporary triumph

The next day, the great crowd who had come to the festival 12
heard that Jesus was coming into Jerusalem, and went out to meet 13
him with palm branches in their hands, shouting, "God save
him! God bless the man who comes in the name of the Lord,
God bless the king of Israel!"

For Jesus had found a young ass and was seated upon it, just 14
as the scripture foretold –

Fear not, daughter of Zion: behold, thy king cometh, sitting 15
on an ass's colt.

(The disciples did not realise the significance of what was happen- 16
ing at the time, but when Jesus was glorified, then they recol-
lected that these things had been written about him and that they
had carried them out for him.)

The people who had been with him, when he had summoned 17
Lazarus from the grave and raised him from the dead, were
continually talking about him. This accounts for the crowd who 18
went out to meet him, for they had heard that he had given this
sign. Seeing all this, the Pharisees remarked to one another, "You 19
see? – There's nothing one can do! The whole world is running
after him."

Among those who had come up to worship at the festival were 20
some Greeks. They approached Philip (whose home town was 21
Bethsaida in Galilee) with the request, "Sir, we want to see Jesus."

Philip went and told Andrew, and Andrew went with Philip 22
and told Jesus.

Jesus told them, "The time has come for the Son of Man to be 23
glorified. I tell you truly that unless a grain of wheat falls into the 24
earth and dies, it remains a single grain of wheat; but if it dies, it
brings a good harvest. The man who loves his own life will 25
destroy it, and the man who hates his life in this world will
preserve it for eternal life. If a man wants to enter my service, 26
he must follow my way; and where I am, my servant will
also be. And my Father will honour every man who enters my
service.

"Now comes my hour of heart-break, and what can I say, 27
'Father, save me from this hour'? No, it was for this very purpose
that I came to this hour. 'Father, honour your own name!'" 28

D   49

At this there came a voice from Heaven, "I have honoured it and I will honour it again!"

29 When the crowd of bystanders heard this, they said it thundered, but some of them said, "An angel spoke to him."

30 Then Jesus said, "That voice came for your sake, not for mine.
31 Now is the time for the judgement of this world to begin, and
32 now will the spirit that rules this world be driven out. As for me, if I am lifted up from the earth, I will draw all men to myself."
33 (He said this to show the kind of death he was going to die.)

34 Then the crowd said, "We have heard from the Law that Christ lives for ever. How can you say that the Son of Man must be 'lifted up'? Who is this Son of Man?"

35 At this, Jesus said to them, "You have the light with you only a little while longer. Go on while the light is good, before the darkness comes down upon you. For the man who walks in
36 the dark has no idea where he is going. You must believe in the light while you have the light, that you may become the sons of light."

Jesus said all these things, and then went away, out of their
37 sight. But though he had given so many signs, yet they did not
38 believe in him, so that the prophecy of Isaiah was fulfilled, when he said,

> Lord, who hath believed our report?
> And to whom hath the arm of the Lord been revealed?

39 Thus, they could not believe, for Isaiah said again –
40 He hath blinded their eyes, and he hardened their heart:
> Lest they should see with their eyes, and perceive with
>   their heart,
> And should turn,
> And I should heal them.

41 Isaiah said these things because he saw the glory of Christ, and
42 spoke about him. Nevertheless, many even of the authorities did believe in him. But they would not admit it for fear of the
43 Pharisees, in case they should be excommunicated. They were more concerned to have the approval of men than to have the approval of God.

44 But later, Jesus cried aloud, "Every man who believes in me,
45 is believing in the one who sent me; and every man who sees
46 me is seeing the one who sent me. I have come into the world as

light, so that no one who believes in me need remain in the dark. Yet, if anyone hears my sayings and does not keep them, I do not judge him – for I did not come to judge the world but to save it. 47 Every man who rejects me and will not accept my sayings has a judge – at the last day, the very words that I have spoken will be 48 his judge. For I have not spoken on my own authority: the Father who sent me has commanded me what to say and what to speak. 49 And I know that what he commands means eternal life. All that I say I speak only in accordance with what the Father has told 50 me."

CHAPTER XIII

Jesus teaches his disciples humility

BEFORE the festival of the Passover began, Jesus realised that the 1 time had come for him to leave this world and return to the Father. He had loved those who were his own in this world and he loved them to the end. By supper-time, the devil had already 2 put the thought of betraying Jesus into the mind of Judas Iscariot, Simon's son. Jesus, with the full knowledge that the Father had 3 put everything into his hands and that he had come from God and was going to God, rose from the supper-table, took off 4 his outer clothes, picked up a towel and fastened it round his waist. Then he poured water into the basin and began to wash 5 the disciples' feet and to dry them with the towel around his waist.

So he came to Simon Peter, who said to him, "Lord, are you 6 going to wash my feet?"

"You do not realise now what I am doing," replied Jesus, "but 7 later on you will understand."

Then Peter said to him, "You must never wash my feet!" 8

"Unless you let me wash you, Peter," replied Jesus, "you cannot share my lot."

"Then," returned Simon Peter, "please – not just my feet but 9 my hands and my face as well!"

10   "The man who has bathed," returned Jesus, "only needs to wash his feet to be clean all over. And you are clean – though not all of you."

11   (For Jesus knew his betrayer and that is why he said, "though not all of you".)

12   When Jesus had washed their feet and put on his clothes, he sat down again and spoke to them, "Do you realise what I have just
13 done to you? You call me 'teacher' and 'Lord' and you are quite
14 right, for I am your teacher and your Lord. But if I, your teacher and Lord, have washed your feet, you must be ready to wash one
15 another's feet. I have given you this as an example so that you
16 may do as I have done. Believe me, the servant is not greater than his master and the messenger is not greater than the man
17 who sent him. Once you have realised these things, you will find your happiness in doing them.

Jesus foretells his betrayal

18   "I am not speaking about all of you – I know the men I have chosen. But let this scripture be fulfilled –
    He that eateth my bread lifted up his heel against me.
19 From now onwards, I shall tell you about things before they happen, so that when they do happen, you may believe that I
20 am the one I claim to be. I tell you truly that anyone who accepts my messenger will be accepting me, and anyone who accepts me will be accepting the one who sent me."

21   After Jesus had said this, he was clearly in anguish of soul, and he added solemnly,
    "I tell you plainly, one of you is going to betray me."

22   At this the disciples stared at each other, completely mystified
23 as to whom he could mean. And it happened that one of them,
24 whom Jesus loved, was sitting very close to him. So Simon Peter nodded to this man and said, "Tell us who he means."

25   He simply leaned forward on Jesus' shoulder, and asked, "Lord, who is it?"

26   And Jesus answered, "It is the one I am going to give this piece of bread to, after I have dipped it in the dish."
    Then he took a piece of bread, dipped it in the dish and gave
27 it to Simon's son, Judas Iscariot. After he had taken the piece of

bread, Satan entered his heart. Then Jesus said to him, "Be quick about your business!"

No one else at table knew what he meant in telling him this. 28 Indeed, some of them thought that, since Judas had charge of 29 the purse, Jesus was telling him to buy what they needed for the festival, or that he should give something to the poor. So 30 Judas took the piece of bread and went out quickly – into the night.

When he had gone, Jesus spoke, "Now comes the glory of the 31 Son of Man, and the glory of God in him! If God is glorified 32 through him then God will glorify the Son of Man – and that without delay. Oh, my children, I am with you such a short 33 time! You will look for me and I have to tell you as I told the Jews, 'Where I am going, you cannot follow.' Now I am giving 34 you a new command – love one another. Just as I have loved you, so you must love one another. This is how all men will know 35 that you are my disciples, because you have such love for one another."

Simon Peter said to him, "Lord, where are you going?" 36

"I am going," replied Jesus, "where you cannot follow me now, though you will follow me later."

"Lord, why can't I follow you now?" said Peter. "I would lay 37 down my life for you!"

"Would you lay down your life for me?" replied Jesus. "Be- 38 lieve me, you will disown me three times before the cock crows!"

CHAPTER XIV

Jesus reveals spiritual truths

"YOU must not let yourselves be distressed – you must hold on 1 to your faith in God and to your faith in me. There are many 2 rooms in my Father's House. If there were not, should I have told you that I am going away to prepare a place for you? It is true 3 that I am going away to prepare a place for you, but it is just as true that I am coming again to welcome you into my own home,

4 so that you may be where I am. You know where I am going and you know the road I am going to take."

5 "Lord," Thomas remonstrated, "we do not know where you're going, and how can we know what road you're going to take?"

6 "I myself am the road," replied Jesus, "and the truth and the
7 life. No one approaches the Father except through me. If you had known who I am, you would have known my Father. From now on, you do know him and you have seen him."

Jesus explains his relationship with the Father

8 Then Philip said to him, "Show us the Father, Lord, and we shall be satisfied."

9 "Have I been such a long time with you," returned Jesus, "without your really knowing me, Philip? The man who has seen me has seen the Father. How can you say, 'Show us the Father'?
10 Do you not believe that I am in the Father and the Father is in me? The very words I say to you are not my own. It is the Father
11 who lives in me who carries out his work through me. Do you believe me when I say that I am in the Father and the Father is in me? But if you cannot, then believe me because of what you
12 see me do. I assure you that the man who believes in me will do the same things that I have done, yes, and he will do even greater
13 things than these, for I am going away to the Father. Whatever you ask the Father in my name, I will do – that the Son may
14 bring glory to the Father. And if you ask me anything in my name, I will grant it.

Jesus promises the Spirit

15 "If you really love me, you will keep the commandments I
16 have given you and I shall ask the Father to give you someone
17 else to stand by you, to be with you always. I mean the Spirit of truth, whom the world cannot accept, for it can neither see nor recognise that Spirit. But you recognise him, for he is with you
18 now and will be in your hearts. I am not going to leave you alone
19 in the world – I am coming to you. In a very little while, the world will see me no more but you will see me, because I am

really alive and you will be alive too. When that day comes, you 20
will realise that I am in my Father, that you are in me, and I am
in you.

"Every man who knows my commandments and obeys them 21
is the man who really loves me, and every man who really loves
me will himself be loved by my Father, and I too will love him
and make myself known to him."

Then Judas (not Iscariot) said, "Lord, how is it that you are 22
going to make yourself known to us but not to the world?"

And to this Jesus replied, "When a man loves me, he follows 23
my teaching. Then my Father will love him, and we will come
to that man and make our home within him. The man who does 24
not really love me will not follow my teaching. Indeed, what you
are hearing from me now is not really my saying, but comes from
the Father who sent me.

"I have said all this while I am still with you. But the one who 25, 26
is coming to stand by you, the Holy Spirit whom the Father will
send in my name, will be your teacher and will bring to your
minds all that I have said to you.

"I leave behind with you – peace; I give you my own peace 27
and my gift is nothing like the peace of this world. You must not
be distressed and you must not be daunted. You have heard me 28
say, 'I am going away and I am coming back to you.' If you really
loved me, you would be glad because I am going to my Father,
for my Father is greater than I. And I have told you of it now, 29
before it happens, so that when it does happen, your faith in me
will not be shaken. I shall not be able to talk much longer to you, 30
for the spirit that rules this world is coming very close. He has no
hold over me, but I go on my way to show the world that I love 31
the Father and do what he sent me to do. . . . Get up now! Let
us leave this place.

CHAPTER XV

Jesus teaches union with himself

1, 2 "I AM the real vine, my Father is the vine-dresser. He removes any of my branches which are not bearing fruit and he prunes
3 every branch that does bear fruit to increase its yield. Now, you
4 have already been pruned by my words. You must go on growing in me and I will grow in you. For just as the branch cannot bear any fruit unless it shares the life of the vine, so you can produce
5 nothing unless you go on growing in me. I am the vine itself, you are the branches. It is the man who shares my life and whose life I share who proves fruitful. For the plain fact is that apart from
6 me you can do nothing at all. The man who does not share my life is like a branch that is broken off and withers away. He becomes just like the dry sticks that men pick up and use for fire-
7 wood. But if you live your life in me, and my words live in your hearts, you can ask for whatever you like and it will come true
8 for you. This is how my Father will be glorified – in your becoming fruitful and being my disciples.

9 "I have loved you just as the Father has loved me. You must
10 go on living in my love. If you keep my commandments you will live in my love just as I have kept my Father's command-
11 ments and live in his love. I have told you this so that you can
12 share my joy, and that your happiness may be complete. This is my commandment: that you love each other as I have loved you.
13 There is no greater love than this – that a man should lay down
14 his life for his friends. You are my friends if you do what I tell you
15 to do. I shall not call you servants any longer, for a servant does not share his master's confidence. No, I call you friends, now, because I have told you everything that I have heard from the Father.

16 "It is not that you have chosen me; but it is I who have chosen you. I have appointed you to go and bear fruit that will be lasting; so that whatever you ask the Father in my name, he will give it to you.

Jesus speaks of the world's hatred

"This I command you, love one another! If the world hates 17, 18
you, you know that it hated me first. If you belonged to the   19
world, the world would love its own. But because you do not
belong to the world and I have chosen you out of it, the world
will hate you. Do you remember what I said to you, 'The servant   20
is not greater than his master'? If they have persecuted me, they
will persecute you as well, but if they have followed my teaching,
they will also follow yours. They will do all these things to you   21
as my disciples because they do not know the one who sent me.
If I had not come and spoken to them, they would not have been   22
guilty of sin, but now they have no excuse for their sin. The man   23
who hates me, hates my Father as well. If I had not done among   24
them things that no other man has ever done, they would not
have been guilty of sin, but as it is they have seen and they have
hated both me and my Father. Yet this only fulfils what is written   25
in their Law –

They hated me without a cause.

But when the helper comes, that is, the Spirit of truth, who comes   26
from the Father and whom I myself will send to you from the
Father, he will speak plainly about me. And you yourselves will   27
also speak plainly about me for you have been with me from the
first."

CHAPTER XVI

Jesus speaks of the future without his bodily presence

"I AM telling you this now so that your faith in me may not be   1
shaken. They will excommunicate you from their synagogues.   2
Yes, the time is coming when a man who kills you will think he
is thereby serving God! They will act like this because they have   3
never had any true knowledge of the Father or of me, but I have   4
told you all this so that when the time comes for it to happen you
may remember that I told you about it. I have not spoken like

57

5 this to you before, because I have been with you; but now the
time has come for me to go away to the one who sent me. None
6 of you asks me, 'Where are you going?' That is because you are
7 so distressed at what I have told you. Yet I am telling you the
simple truth when I assure you that it is a good thing for you
that I should go away. For if I did not go away, the divine
helper would not come to you. But if I go, then I will send
8 him to you. When he comes, he will convince the world of
9 the meaning of sin, of true goodness and of judgement. He will
10 expose their sin because they do not believe in me; he will
reveal true goodness, for I am going away to the Father and you
11 will see me no longer; and he will show them the meaning of
judgement, for the spirit which rules this world will have been
judged.

12 "I have much more to tell you but you cannot bear it now.
13 Yet when that one I have spoken to you about comes – the Spirit
of truth – he will guide you into everything that is true. For
he will not be speaking of his own accord but exactly as he
14 hears, and he will inform you about what is to come. He will
bring glory to me, for he will draw on my truth and reveal it
15 to you. Whatever the Father possesses is also mine; that is why
I tell you that he will draw on my truth and will show it to
you.

The disciples are puzzled: Jesus explains

16 "In a little while you will not see me any longer, and again,
in a little while you will see me."
17 At this some of his disciples remarked to each other, "What is
this that he tells us now, 'A little while and you will not see
me, and again, in a little while you will see me' and 'for I am
18 going away to the Father'? What is this 'little while' that he talks
about?" they were saying. "We simply do not know what he
means!"
19 Jesus knew that they wanted to ask him what he meant, so he
said to them, "Are you trying to find out from each other what I
meant when I said, 'In a little while you will not see me, and
20 again, in a little while you will see me'? I tell you truly that you
are going to be both sad and sorry while the world is glad. Yes,

you will be deeply distressed, but your pain will turn into joy. When a woman gives birth to a child, she certainly knows pain *21* when her time comes. Yet as soon as she has given birth to the child, she no longer remembers her agony for joy that a man has been born into the world. Now you are going through pain, but *22* I shall see you again and your hearts will thrill with joy – the joy that no one can take away from you – and on that day you will *23* not ask me any questions.

"I assure you that whatever you ask the Father he will give you in my name. Up to now you have asked nothing in my *24* name; ask now, and you will receive, that your joy may be over-flowing.

Jesus speaks further of the future

"I have been speaking to you in parables – but the time is *25* coming to give up parables and tell you plainly about the Father. When that time comes, you will make your requests to him in *26* my name, for I need make no promise to plead to the Father for you, for the Father himself loves you, because you have loved *27* me and have believed that I came from God. Yes, I did come *28* from the Father and I came into the world. Now I leave the world behind and return to the Father."

"Now you are speaking plainly," cried the disciples, "and are *29* not using parables. Now we know that everything is known to *30* you – no more questions are needed. This makes us sure that you did come from God."

"So you believe in me now?" replied Jesus. "The time is *31, 32* coming, indeed, it has already come, when you will be scattered, every one of you going home and leaving me alone. Yet I am not really alone, for the Father is with me. I have told you all *33* this so that you may find your peace in me. You will find trouble in the world – but, never lose heart, I have conquered the world!"

CHAPTER XVII

Jesus' prayer for his disciples – present and future

1 WHEN Jesus had said these words, he raised his eyes to Heaven and said, "Father, the hour has come. Glorify your Son now so
2 that he may bring glory to you, for you have given him authority over all men to give eternal life to all that you have given to him.
3 And this is eternal life, to know you, the only true God, and him whom you have sent – Jesus Christ.

4 "I have brought you honour upon earth, I have completed the
5 task which you gave me to do. Now, Father, honour me in your own presence with the glory that I knew with you before the
6 world was made. I have shown your self to the men whom you gave me from the world. They were your men and you gave
7 them to me, and they have accepted your word. Now they realise
8 that all that you have given me comes from you – and that every message that you gave me I have given them. They have accepted it all and have come to know in their hearts that I did come from you – they are convinced that you sent me.

9 "I am praying to you for them: I am not praying for the world
10 but for the men whom you gave me, for they are yours – everything that is mine is yours and yours mine – and they have done
11 me honour. Now I am no longer in the world, but they are in the world and I am returning to you. Holy Father, keep the men you gave me by your power that they may be one, as we are one.
12 As long as I was with them, I kept them by the power that you gave me; I guarded them, and not one of them was destroyed, except the son of destruction – that the scripture might come true.

13 "And now I come to you and I say these things in the world
14 that these men may find my joy completed in themselves. I have given them your word, and the world has hated them, for they
15 are no more sons of the world than I am. I am not praying that you will take them out of the world but that you will keep them
16 from the evil one. They are no more the sons of the world than
17 I am – make them holy by the truth; for your word is the truth.
18, 19 I have sent them to the world just as you sent me to the world and

60

I consecrate myself for their sakes that they may be made holy by the truth.

"I am not praying only for these men but for all those who will 20 believe in me through their message, that they may all be one. 21 Just as you, Father, live in me and I live in you, I am asking that they may live in us, that the world may believe that you did send me. I have given them the honour that you gave me, that 22 they may be one, as we are one – I in them and you in me, that 23 they may grow complete into one, so that the world may realise that you sent me and have loved them as you loved me. Father, 24 I want those whom you have given me to be with me where I am; I want them to see that glory which you have made mine – for you loved me before the world began. Father of goodness and 25 truth, the world has not known you, but I have known you and these men now know that you have sent me. I have made your 26 self known to them and I will continue to do so that the love which you have had for me may be in their hearts – and that I may be there also."

CHAPTER XVIII

Jesus is arrested in the garden

WHEN Jesus had spoken these words, he went out with his 1 disciples across the Cedron valley to a place where there was a garden, and they went into it together. Judas who betrayed him 2 knew the place, for Jesus often met his disciples there. So Judas 3 fetched the guard and the officers which the chief priests and Pharisees had provided for him, and came to the place with torches and lanterns and weapons. Jesus, fully realising all that 4 was going to happen to him, went forward and said to them, "Who are you looking for?"

"Jesus of Nazareth," they answered. 5

"I am the man," said Jesus. (Judas who was betraying him was standing there with the others.)

When he said to them, "I am the man", they retreated and fell 6

7 to the ground. So Jesus asked them again, "Who are you looking for?"

And again they said, "Jesus of Nazareth."

8 "I have told you that I am the man," replied Jesus. "If I am
9 the man you are looking for, let these others go." (Thus fulfilling his previous words, "I have not lost one of those whom you gave me.")

10 At this, Simon Peter, who had a sword, drew it and slashed at the High Priest's servant, cutting off his right ear. (The servant's
11 name was Malchus.) But Jesus said to Peter, "Put your sword back into its sheath. Am I not to drink the cup the Father has given me?"

Peter follows Jesus, only to deny him

12 Then the guard, with their captain and the Jewish officers, took
13 hold of Jesus and tied his hands together, and led him off to Annas first, for he was father-in-law to Caiaphas, who was High
14 Priest that year. Caiaphas was the man who advised the Jews, "that it would be a good thing that one man should die for the
15 sake of the people". Behind Jesus followed Simon Peter, and one other disciple who was known personally to the High Priest. He
16 went in with Jesus into the High Priest's courtyard, but Peter was left standing at the door outside. So this other disciple, who was acquainted with the High Priest, went out and spoke to the door-
17 keeper, and brought Peter inside. The young woman at the door remarked to Peter, "Are you one of this man's disciples, too?"

"No, I am not," retorted Peter.

18 In the courtyard, the servants and officers stood around a char-coal fire which they had made, for it was cold. They were warming themselves, and Peter stood there with them, keeping himself warm.

19 Meanwhile the High Priest interrogated Jesus about his disciples and about his own teaching.

20 "I have always spoken quite openly to the world," replied Jesus. "I have always taught in the synagogue or in the Temple where all Jews meet together, and I have said nothing in secret.
21 Why do you question me? Why not question those who have

heard me about what I said to them? Obviously they are the ones who know what I actually said."

As he said this, one of those present, an officer, slapped Jesus with his open hand, remarking, "Is that the way for you to answer the High Priest?" 22

"If I have said anything wrong," Jesus said to him, "you must give evidence about it, but if what I said was true, why do you strike me?" 23

Then Annas sent him, with his hands still tied, to the High Priest Caiaphas. 24

Peter's denial

In the meantime Simon Peter was still standing, keeping himself warm. Some of them said to him, "Surely you too are one of his disciples, aren't you?" 25

And he denied it and said, "No, I am not."

Then one of the High Priest's servants, a relation of the man whose ear Peter had cut off, remarked, "Didn't I see you in the garden with him?" 26

And again Peter denied it. And immediately the cock crew. 27

Jesus is taken before the Roman authority

Then they led Jesus from Caiaphas' presence into the palace. It was now early morning and the Jews themselves did not go into the palace, for fear that they would be contaminated and would not be able to eat the Passover. So Pilate walked out to them and said, "What is the charge that you are bringing against this man?" 28

29

"If he were not an evil-doer, we should not have handed him over to you," they replied. 30

To which Pilate retorted, "Then take him yourselves and judge him according to your law." 31

"We are not allowed to put a man to death," replied the Jews (thus fulfilling Christ's prophecy of the method of his own death). 32

So Pilate went back into the Palace and called Jesus to him. "Are you the king of the Jews?" he asked. 33

34   "Are you asking this of your own accord," replied Jesus, "or have other people spoken to you about me?"

35   "Do you think *I* am a Jew?" replied Pilate. "It's your people and your chief priests who handed you over to me. What have you done, anyway?"

36   "My kingdom is not founded in this world – if it were, my servants would have fought to prevent my being handed over to the Jews. But in fact my kingdom is not founded on all this!"

37   "So you are a king, are you?" returned Pilate.

"Indeed I am a king," Jesus replied; "the reason for my birth and the reason for my coming into the world is to witness to the truth. Every man who loves truth recognises my voice."

38   To which Pilate retorted, "What is 'truth'?" and went straight out again to the Jews and said:

39   "I find nothing criminal about him at all. But I have an arrangement with you to set one prisoner free at Passover time. Do you wish me then to set free for you the 'king of the Jews'?"

40   At this, they shouted out again, "No, not this man, but Barabbas!"

Barabbas was a bandit.

CHAPTER XIX

Pilate's vain efforts to save Jesus

1, 2   THEN Pilate took Jesus and had him flogged, and the soldiers twisted thorn-twigs into a crown and put it on his head, threw

3   a purple robe around him and kept coming into his presence, saying, "Hail, king of the Jews!" And then they slapped him with their open hands.

4   Then Pilate went outside again and said to them, "Look, I bring him out before you here, to show that I find nothing criminal about him at all."

5   And at this Jesus came outside too, wearing the thorn crown and the purple robe.

"Look," said Pilate, "here's the man!"

The sight of him made the chief priests and Jewish officials 6
shout at the top of their voices, "Crucify! Crucify!"

"You take him and crucify him," retorted Pilate. "He's no
criminal as far as I can see!"

The Jews answered him, "We have a Law, and according to 7
that Law, he must die, for he made himself out to be Son of
God!"

When Pilate heard them say this, he became much more un- 8
easy, and returned to the palace again and spoke to Jesus, "Where 9
do you come from?"

But Jesus gave him no reply. So Pilate said to him, "Won't 10
you speak to me? Don't you realise that I have the power to set
you free, and I have the power to have you crucified?"

"You have no power at all against me," replied Jesus, "except 11
what was given to you from above. And for that reason the one
who handed me over to you is even more guilty than you are."

From that moment, Pilate tried hard to set him free but the 12
Jews were shouting, "If you set this man free, you are no friend
of Caesar! Anyone who makes himself out to be a king is anti-
Caesar!"

When Pilate heard this, he led Jesus outside and sat down upon 13
the Judgement-seat in the place called the Pavement (in Hebrew,
Gabbatha). It was the preparation day of the Passover and it was 14
now getting on towards midday. Pilate now said to the Jews,
"Look, here's your king!"

At which they yelled, "Take him away, take him away, 15
crucify him!"

"Am I to crucify your king?" Pilate asked them.

"Caesar is our king and no one else," replied the chief priests.
And at this Pilate handed Jesus over to them for crucifixion. 16

The crucifixion

So they took Jesus and he went out carrying the cross himself, 17
to a place called Skull Hill (in Hebrew, Golgotha). There they 18
crucified him, and two others, one on either side of him with Jesus
in the middle. Pilate had a placard written out and put on the 19
cross, reading, JESUS OF NAZARETH, THE KING OF

E

20 THE JEWS. This placard was read by many of the Jews because the place where Jesus was crucified was quite near Jerusalem, and
21 it was written in Hebrew as well as in Latin and Greek. So the chief priests said to Pilate, "You should not write 'The King of the Jews', but 'This man said, I am King of the Jews.'"
22 To which Pilate retorted, "Indeed? What I have written, I have written."
23 When the soldiers had crucified Jesus, they divided his clothes between them, taking a quarter-share each. There remained his shirt, which was seamless – woven in one piece from the top to
24 the bottom. So they said to each other, "Don't let us tear it; let's draw lots and see who gets it."
This happened to fulfil the scripture which says –

They parted my garments among them,
And upon my vesture did they cast lots.

Jesus provides for his mother from the cross

25 While the soldiers were doing this, Jesus' mother was standing near the cross with her sister, and with them Mary, the wife of
26 Clopas, and Mary of Magdala. Jesus saw his mother and the disciple whom he loved standing by her side, and said to her,
27 "Look, there is your son!" And then he said to the disciple, "And there is your mother!"
And from that time the disciple took Mary into his own home.
28 After this, Jesus realising that everything was now completed, said (fulfilling the saying of scripture), "I am thirsty."
29 There was a bowl of sour wine standing there. So they soaked a sponge in the wine, put it on a spear, and pushed it up towards
30 his mouth. When Jesus had taken it, he cried, "It is finished!" his head fell forward, and he died.

The body of Jesus is removed

31 As it was the day of preparation for the Passover, the Jews wanted to avoid the bodies being left on the crosses over the Sabbath (for that was a particularly important Sabbath), and they requested Pilate to have the men's legs broken and the bodies

removed. So the soldiers went and broke the legs of the first man   *32*
and of the other who was crucified with Jesus. But when they   *33*
came to him, they saw that he was dead already and they did
not break his legs. But one of the soldiers pierced his side with a   *34*
spear, and at once there was an outrush of blood and water. And   *35*
the man who saw this is our witness: his evidence is true. (He is
certain that he is speaking the truth, so that you may believe as
well.) For this happened to fulfil the scripture,   *36*
    A bone of him shall not be broken.
And again another scripture says –   *37*
    They shall look on him whom they pierced.

After it was all over, Joseph (who came from Arimathaea and   *38*
was a disciple of Jesus, though secretly for fear of the Jews) requested Pilate that he might take away Jesus' body, and Pilate
gave him permission. So he came and took his body down.
Nicodemus also, the man who had come to him at the beginning   *39*
by night, arrived bringing a mixture of myrrh and aloes, weigh-
ing about a hundred pounds. So they took his body and wound   *40*
it round with linen strips with the spices, according to the Jewish
custom of preparing a body for burial. In the place where he was   *41*
crucified, there was a garden containing a new tomb in which
nobody had yet been laid. Because it was the preparation day and   *42*
because the tomb was conveniently near, they laid Jesus in this
tomb.

CHAPTER XX

The first day of the week: the risen Lord

BUT on the first day of the week, Mary of Magdala arrived at   *1*
the tomb, very early in the morning, while it was still dark, and
noticed that the stone had been taken away from the tomb. At   *2*
this she ran, found Simon Peter and the other disciple whom Jesus
loved, and told them, "They have taken the Lord out of the tomb
and we don't know where they have put him."

Peter and the other disciple set off at once for the tomb, the   *3*

4 two of them running together. The other disciple ran faster than
5 Peter and was the first to arrive at the tomb. He stooped and
looked inside and noticed the linen cloths lying there but did not
6 go in himself. Hard on his heels came Simon Peter and went
straight into the tomb. He noticed that the linen cloths were
7 lying there, and that the handkerchief, which had been round
Jesus' head, was not lying with the linen cloths but was rolled
8 up by itself, a little way apart. Then the other disciple, who was
the first to arrive at the tomb, came inside as well, saw what
9 had happened and believed. (They did not yet understand the
10 scripture which said that he must rise from the dead.) So the disciples went back again to their homes.

11 But Mary stood just outside the tomb, and she was crying. And
12 as she cried, she looked into the tomb and saw two angels in white
who sat, one at the head and the other at the foot of the place
where the body of Jesus had lain.

13 The angels spoke to her, "Why are you crying?" they asked.
"Because they have taken away my Lord, and I don't know
where they have put him!" she said.

14 Then she turned and noticed Jesus standing there, without
realising that it was Jesus.

15 "Why are you crying?" said Jesus to her. "Who are you
looking for?"

She, supposing that he was the gardener, said, "Oh, sir, if you
have carried him away, please tell me where you have put him
and I will take him away."

16 Jesus said to her, "Mary!"

At this she turned right round and said to him, in Hebrew,
"Master!"

17 "No!" said Jesus, "do not hold me now. I have not yet gone
up to the Father. Go and tell my brothers that I am going up to
my Father and your Father, to my God and your God."

18 And Mary of Magdala went off to the disciples, with the news,
"I have seen the Lord!", and she told them what he had said to
her.

19 In the evening of that first day of the week, the disciples had
met together with the doors locked for fear of the Jews. Jesus
came and stood right in the middle of them and said, "Peace be
with you!"

Then he showed them his hands and his side, and when they 20
saw the Lord the disciples were overjoyed.

Jesus said to them again, "Yes, peace be with you! Just as the 21
Father sent me, so I am now going to send you."

And then he breathed upon them and said, "Receive holy 22
spirit.* If you forgive any men's sins, they are forgiven, and if 23
you hold them unforgiven, they are unforgiven."

The risen Jesus and Thomas

But one of the twelve, Thomas (called the Twin), was not 24
with them when Jesus came. The other disciples kept on telling 25
him, "We have seen the Lord", but he replied, "Unless I see in
his own hands the mark of the nails, and put my finger where the
nails were, and put my hand into his side, I will never believe!"

Just over a week later, the disciples were indoors again and 26
Thomas was with them. The doors were shut, but Jesus came and
stood in the middle of them and said, "Peace be with you!"

Then he said to Thomas, "Put your finger here – look, here 27
are my hands. Take your hand and put it in my side. You must
not doubt, but believe."

"My Lord and my God!" cried Thomas. 28

"Is it because you have seen me that you believe?" Jesus said 29
to him. "Happy are those who have never seen me and yet have
believed!"

Jesus gave a great many other signs in the presence of his 30
disciples which are not recorded in this book. But these have been 31
written so that you may believe that Jesus is Christ, the Son of
God, and that in that faith you may have life as his disciples.

* Lit. "receive holy spirit". Historically the Holy Spirit was not given until
Pentecost.

CHAPTER XXI

The risen Jesus and Peter

1 LATER on, Jesus showed himself again to his disciples on the
2 shore of Lake Tiberias, and he did it in this way. Simon Peter.
Thomas (called the Twin), Nathanael from Cana of Galilee, the
3 sons of Zebedee and two other disciples were together, when
Simon Peter said,

"I'm going fishing."

"All right," they replied, "we'll go with you."

So they went out and got into the boat and during the night
4 caught nothing at all. But just as dawn began to break, Jesus stood
there on the beach, although the disciples had no idea that it was
Jesus.

5 "Have you caught anything, lads?" Jesus called out to them.
"No," they replied.

6 "Throw the net on the right side of the boat," said Jesus, "and
you'll have a catch."

So they threw out the net and found that they were now
7 not strong enough to pull it in because it was so full of fish!
At this, the disciple that Jesus loved said to Peter, "It is the
Lord!"

Hearing this, Peter slipped on his clothes, for he had been
8 naked, and plunged into the sea. The other disciples followed in
the boat, for they were only about a hundred yards from the
9 shore, dragging in the net full of fish. When they had landed,
they saw that a charcoal fire was burning, with a fish placed on
10 it, and some bread. Jesus said to them, "Bring me some of the fish
you've just caught."

11 So Simon Peter got into the boat and hauled the net ashore full
of large fish, one hundred and fifty-three altogether. But in spite
of the large number the net was not torn.

12 Then Jesus said to them, "Come and have your breakfast."

None of the disciples dared to ask him who he was; they knew
it was the Lord.

13 Jesus went and took the bread and gave it to them and gave

them all fish as well. This is already the third time that Jesus 14
showed himself to his disciples after his resurrection from the
dead.

When they had finished breakfast Jesus said to Simon Peter, 15
"Simon, son of John, do you love me more than these others?"

"Yes, Lord," he replied, "you know that I am your friend."

"Then feed my lambs," returned Jesus. Then he said for the 16
second time,

"Simon, son of John, do you love me?"

"Yes, Lord," returned Peter. "You know that I am your
friend."

"Then care for my sheep," replied Jesus. Then for the third 17
time, Jesus spoke to him and said,

"Simon, son of John, *are* you my friend?"

Peter was deeply hurt because Jesus' third question to him was
"Are you my friend?", and he said, "Lord, you know everything.
You know that I am your friend!"

"Then feed my sheep," Jesus said to him. "I tell you truly, 18
Peter, that when you were younger, you used to dress yourself
and go where you liked, but when you are an old man, you are
going to stretch out your hands and someone else will dress you
and take you where you do not want to go."

(He said this to show the kind of death by which Peter was 19
going to honour God.)

Then Jesus said to him, "You must follow me."

Then Peter turned round and noticed the disciple whom Jesus 20
loved following behind them. (He was the one who had his head
on Jesus' shoulder at supper and had asked, "Lord, who is the
one who is going to betray you?") So he said, "Yes, Lord, but 21
what about him?"

"If it is my wish," returned Jesus, "for him to stay until I 22
come, is that your business, Peter? You must follow me."

This gave rise to the saying among the brothers that this dis- 23
ciple would not die. Yet, of course, Jesus did not say, "He will not
die", but simply, "If it is my wish for him to stay until I come,
is that your business?"

All the above was written by an eye-witness

24 Now it is this same disciple who is hereby giving his testimony
to these things and has written them down. We know that his
25 witness is reliable. Of course, there are many other things which
Jesus did, and I suppose that if each one were written down in
detail, there would not be room in the whole world for all the
books that would have to be written.

CONTENTS OF THE HISTORICAL COMMENTARY

I. 19–51. The ministry of Jesus follows and arises from the Baptist's prior ministry. The latter, claiming no more for himself than that he was "a voice crying in the desert", declared that he would be followed by another, a greater than he, whom he may well have called "God's Chosen One". We need not accept the view of many scholars that it was by his mission alone, and not by any insight, that the Baptist pointed to Jesus, but John II's account of the meeting of Jesus and the Baptist cannot, as it stands, be accurate. Whatever be the meaning of the obscure title, "the Lamb of God"*, we cannot suppose that from the first the Baptist declared Jesus to be the Lamb of God who takes away the sin of the world or applied to him the very odd phrase translated, or rather paraphrased, in *The New English Bible* as "a man who takes rank before me; for before I was born, he already was" (v. 30). As little can we believe that Andrew already recognised Jesus as the Messiah of Jewish hope (v. 41). Such phrases must be taken as Johannine theology and as excellently illustrating John II's method. If, as he supposed, Jesus was really he who should take away the sin of the world, the Word incarnate, the Messiah of the Jews, then the Baptist or Andrew in pointing to Jesus was in fact, though not consciously, pointing to the figure of John II's theology.

There is, however, good reason for surmising that John I himself was present when the Baptist spoke of Jesus, for two of the Baptist's disciples, we read, thereupon followed Jesus and asked him where he was staying. Jesus told them to come and see. It was about four o'clock in the afternoon (v. 39). One of these two was Andrew; the other is not named, but since in the gathering of these first disciples of Jesus we are carefully given names, it is reasonable to surmise that John I was himself the unnamed disciple.

The story of these first beginnings is told in briefest form. We must fill it out as best we can by the exercise of imagination. It would, for instance, be unreasonable to suppose that any person applying to John for baptism would at once be dipped in Jordan with no questions asked. We will postulate that John and Jesus

* *v.* C. H. Dodd, *Historical Tradition In The Fourth Gospel*, p. 270.

talked long together. Jesus' estimate of John's mission we are told (Matt. XI. 7; Luke VII. 24; Jno. V. 35), but what did Jesus tell John of that mission of which he himself was conscious? It is permissible, almost necessary, to suppose that the substance of what Jesus said to John was the passage of Scripture which, according to Luke (IV. 18), was the text from which at the very beginning of his ministry he spoke in the synagogue at Nazareth, "The Spirit of the Lord is upon me; wherefore he has anointed me to preach good news to the poor; he has sent me to proclaim release to the captives and sight to the blind, to set free the broken victims, to proclaim the year of the Lord's favour". This we may guess, for we are told that the Baptist was profoundly moved and quickened by what Jesus said to him. When we of the modern psychological world have some deep emotional experience and intellectual enlightenment, we try to express it in such phrases as "it dawned upon me", "I was suddenly aware", "it came to me like a revelation", "I knew it in my heart" and the like. The Hebrews used pictorial, not psychological, terms for the description of their experience; they would say, "I heard the voice of God saying", or "an angel of the Lord appeared unto me saying", or "I saw the Spirit descending like a dove and resting on him". When the Baptist had met Jesus and talked with him and baptised him, he pointed to him and, perhaps addressing only the few who were closely attached to him, he said, "there he is; there is that Other whom I have been predicting, God's Chosen One". This leads to the first collection of disciples, Andrew, Peter, Philip, Nathanael and John himself.

Andrew and John had asked Jesus where he was staying and were told to come and see; they spent the rest of that day with him, and of that long conversation not a word comes down to us. We know only that "first" or, perhaps more probably, next morning, as some Latin mss. suggest, Andrew goes to find his brother Simon. Then Jesus "finds" or "meets" Philip. We naturally assume that Jesus already knew Philip or at least had been told about him by the others. Then Philip finds Nathanael (vv. 37–45).

The story of the encounter between Jesus and Nathanael is to be taken, not as apocryphal, but as illustrating the style and method of John II. The concluding verse (v. 51) concerning the opening of the heavens and the convergence of the angels upon "the Son of Man" seems out of place and inappropriate here; it presupposes that this mysterious term, "the Son of Man", is intelligible and familiar. The verse begins, "he says to him (singular), I tell you (plural), you shall see . . .". Regarding v. 51, then, as Johannine, I shall venture to interpret the story in this way: it was customary, as we know, for Jews to study the Law under a fig tree. Jesus passing by was particularly struck by the face of a man absorbed in the study of the Law; he read his character. Philip, either because he knew Nathanael or because Jesus had instructed him, goes up to him saying, "we have found the man whom the Baptist has been predicting, Joseph's son, Jesus, from Nazareth". Hearing that Jesus comes from Nazareth, a town close to Cana, where he lives, Nathanael is not at all impressed. Philip, however, insists on his coming to be introduced to Jesus. Jesus says to him, "you are not really a stranger to me; I know you". "How can you possibly know me?" asks Nathanael, "I have never seen you before". "I noticed you under the fig tree," answers Jesus. Nathanael, looking into the eyes of Jesus and strangely moved, says, "Rabbi, I believe you are indeed the man to whom the Baptist pointed". Jesus said to him, "do you believe this just because I said I noticed you under the fig tree? You shall see much more than that."

In sum, the Baptist in a moment of spiritual insight points his followers to Jesus. A small group, Andrew, Peter, Philip, Nathanael and, it would seem, John himself, are, as we say, deeply interested and impressed. This is the beginning of the story. It is entirely credible; as we have reason to think, it goes back to the testimony of one of this first group; it is of the stuff of history.

The figure of Jesus has been introduced; it is accompanied by no "miracle"; it is illuminated by no teaching. All that we can see, or can infer, is the immense impression made upon the Baptist, himself "more than a prophet", and upon a few spiritually minded men by their first contact with this mysterious person, Jesus.

II. 1–11. The story of the turning of the water into wine reads like the apocryphal legend that Jesus, the wonder-worker, caused clay birds to fly. C. H. Dodd, who suggests that possibly some parable of Jesus underlies the story, writes that "its central feature appears to be of non-Christian origin".* Modern commentators in general are accordingly interested in the evangelist's intention in the insertion of this story and in its theological significance. I, on the other hand, am testing my theory that John II was not a romancer, that he supposed himself to be reporting what really happened, and that somewhere behind him he had the reminiscences of John I.

John I, who in general neglects Jesus' Galilean ministry, was presumably not present himself at this wedding feast, but he knew the firm tradition that the first 'sign' whereby Jesus manifested his 'glory' was at Cana in Galilee at a wedding party. What really happened?

The story begins quite credibly. Jesus' Mother is at a wedding feast to which Jesus and his companions have also been invited. It comes to his Mother's ears that the wine is giving out; she, conscious of the social disaster or shame which this would involve and the spoiling of the occasion for the bridegroom, the bride and their parents, says to Jesus, "they haven't any more wine". When Jesus addresses her as 'woman', that is not a discourtesy. He says, in effect, "my dear, that is really not our affair; it is no concern of yours and mine". But his Mother, who, no doubt with good reason, has an unlimited confidence in her son's ability to deal with any untoward situation, says to the worried servants, "you do whatever he suggests; he'll find a way of dealing with this", and Jesus, who later could not refuse the appeal of the Syrophoenician woman, certainly cannot refuse his Mother's appeal now.

Up to this point the story is perfectly straightforward and credible. The sequel, as we receive it, is incredible. Not only is such wonder-working wholly 'out of character', but we are asked to believe that by an act of supernatural power Jesus produced (at the lowest estimate) some 120 gallons of wine and thus manifested his 'glory', causing his followers to "believe in him" – to believe in him, presumably, as a thaumaturgist. We can only guess (and that not very profitably) at what really happened. But assuming John I's statement that Jesus first manifested his glory at a wedding feast in Cana, and taking the first part of the story as I have out-

* op. cit. p. 227.

lined it, it is open to us to suppose that Jesus so took the situation
in hand, perhaps by what he said to the assembled guests, that by
general consent, though the wine was much diluted, the conclusion of the feast, far from being a catastrophe, was its climax. In
that case Jesus would really have revealed the 'glory' or wonder or
mysterious power of his person. If something like this occurred, it
would not be easy for those present to explain to others what had
happened, and in the retelling of the story an unexpected incre-
ment of joy could quickly and easily pass into the legendary form
of a miraculous augmentation of the wine. Such a recasting of the
incident is quite unconvincing. It may be of much significance
that the word for "servants" in v. 5 is *diakonoi* or deacons, and
that John II has here in mind the eucharistic wine as in ch. VI the
eucharistic bread. This consideration, however, throws no light
upon what really happened. John II undoubtedly records a
'miracle' but, if my guess, which is indeed only a guess, is near the
truth, we have so far no picture of what Jesus did nor of what he
said but only of the impression of his personality upon those who
met him.

II. 12–22. John I has little to tell us of the Galilean ministry, presumably because he was not generally present. Verse 12 might
seem to suggest that Jesus' Mother had moved her home to
Capernaum, but this we cannot know.

Of the cleansing of the temple (vv. 13–22) John will have spoken
from personal reminiscence. Commentators give theological
reasons why John II places this event at the beginning of the
ministry; he was, to revert to Spenser's language, poet, not
historiographer. The cleansing of the temple almost certainly took
place during Jesus' final appeal to his people in Jerusalem. There
is no need to suppose that John I ever suggested that it took place
earlier.

The spiritual significance of the driving out of the traders and
money-changers is clear enough: "take these things away; you
are not to turn my Father's house into a bazaar"; (v. 16), but the
significance of the event for the understanding of the person of
Jesus may more easily be overlooked. The traffic and trading in the
outer court of the temple was as much a part of the Establishment

as is, for instance, Smithfield market or the Stock Exchange amongst ourselves. We may fairly assume, that in the action he took Jesus had considerable popular support. Even so, how did he manage to get the traders and the money-changers and the animals to clear out? His fierce indignation, his burning words, his whip sufficed. He chucked them out (*exebalen* in the Greek). We have here an indication of the force and magnificence of Jesus' personality, of his speech and of his anger, of his royal authority and courage. Whatever support he may have had, the clearing of the outer court of the temple was the astonishing achievement of a single man.

It was only to be expected that the Sadducees who had a financial interest in the temple trading should have asked him what authority he had for this high-handed action. "Destroy this temple," Jesus replied (v. 19), "and in three days I will raise it up," or, in modern English, "if you were to destroy this temple, I would raise it up again in a few days' time". There is sufficient evidence that Jesus did in fact anticipate and predict the destruction of Jerusalem and its temple (Mark XIII. 2, Luke XXI. 5f.), and a garbled version of his words may have been brought up at his trial (Mark XIV. 58). But if John I is correctly reported here, what could Jesus have been understood to mean?

The narrative, as we receive it from John II, goes on to explain that the Sadducees totally misunderstood Jesus; they (very naturally) thought he was speaking about the temple where they stood; Jesus, on the other hand, was really talking about the temple of his own body which after three days was to be raised from the dead. This is not to be believed. When the Sadducees asked Jesus a very natural and reasonable question, he cannot have replied with a riddle which they could not possibly interpret.

"Destroy this temple, and in a few days I will raise it up again." How could the Sadducees and all who heard it have understood this answer? Many will have taken his words literally, as if he were "claiming a grotesque architectural capacity".* We should do well to assume, however, that he was not only speaking with immense seriousness but also with the intention of being understood. Whenever his authority was challenged, Jesus always refused to give a 'sign', some sign from heaven to vindicate his

* Hoskyns, *ad loc.*

heavenly calling; spiritual things, he said in effect, are spiritually discerned. His answer to the Sadducees on this occasion might be paraphrased or elongated thus: "you are taking the temple too seriously; it is not buildings that matter; the real temple or dwelling place of God is not a temple of stone; it is in the heart of man. If you or the Romans or an earthquake were to destroy this temple, I would build up again God's real temple in a very short time." St Paul, then, may be making direct reference to Jesus' words when he tells the Corinthians that their bodies are the temple of God (I Cor. III. 16. VI. 19).

In fine, Jesus, by the single force of his personality, had cleared the temple courts of the traffickers and money-changers. It seems likely that when challenged to justify his action he declared that if the whole temple were destroyed, he, by his word and teaching and by the manifestation of the power of God, would raise up a spiritual temple to God who is Spirit. What manner of man was this who could so act and so speak in terms so revolutionary and so imperial? We read of the sayings and doings of Jesus with traditional placidity, but if we had seen him clear the temple court and heard him declare that, were the temple destroyed, he would quickly raise up another temple, we, like his contemporaries, should be presented with the inescapable dilemma: Is this man mad? or is his voice the very word of God?

II. 23–25. These verses read like a personal reminiscence. We cannot be certain that they refer to Jesus' last visit to Jerusalem, but it was Passover time, and Jesus had been 'doing signs', by which we should understand that he was actively exercising his ministry of teaching and of healing. Many, we are told, "believed on his name", but he, knowing men's hearts, did not commit himself to them. The Greek might better be represented by saying that many trusted in him, but he did not entrust himself to them.

What is meant by "believing on (or in or, strictly, into) his name"? In Hebrew thought a name was not, as we should say, a mere name; it represented the character and personality of him who bore it. We should understand that this ministry through the days of the Feast created very great interest and excitement and even hope. This strange, authoritative and revolutionary teaching coupled with these 'miracles' of healing seemed to portend some new turn in history. The popularity of Jesus with the common folk was great, but he remained deliberately aloof in the sense of absolutely declining to put himself at the head of any popular movement, for he realised how shallow was the popular understanding of what he meant. This reads like the kind of personal reminiscence which we do not find in the Synoptic Gospels. It reflects, perhaps, the disappointment or frustration of the inner band of Jesus' followers. Was he not throwing away his opportunity?

III. 1–21. It is impossible convincingly to disprove the contention that this story of the conversation with Nicodemus or the miracle of Cana which precedes it, or the story of the woman of Samaria that follows it, is an exercise of John II's imagination to serve his theological interest and evangelical purpose. I am working on the contrary supposition that the Gospel represents in its narratives the genuine reminiscences of an old disciple. Here verses 11–21 are undoubtedly Johannine, but I see no sufficient reason to doubt that verses 1–10 refer to an historical event.

Nicodemus was a member of the Sanhedrin, a Pharisee. It was natural, and presumably inevitable, that wishing for a private conversation with Jesus he should come to him by night. If this was a private meeting, John I was not present at it; he can only have learnt about it from Jesus or from Nicodemus, presumably the latter. The conversation in our account of it is tantalisingly condensed. It is not to be thought that Jesus met Nicodemus's courteous opening remarks with the uncompromising and apparently irrelevant statement that unless a man be born again (or from above) he cannot see the kingdom of God (v. 3). We must elongate the conversation imaginatively if we would make sense of it.

I conceive that Nicodemus brings to Jesus an agonising spiritual problem. He cannot deny that Jesus seems to him a teacher sent by God, and indeed the 'signs' that he wrought* seemed to indicate God's confirmation of his teaching. Nicodemus, on the other hand, was a strict Jew; he had been brought up to believe that if a

* His healing ministry and casting out of evil spirits is here presupposed.

man would be pleasing to God he must gladly take upon him the yoke and burden of the Law, being strictly obedient to its requirements. Yet Jesus' teaching, which did indeed sound in his ears like a word from God himself, was utterly revolutionary in its implications; not only did Jesus say little or nothing about the Law, but he even disregarded it in such elementary matters as the keeping of the sabbath.

To this Jesus would seem to have replied, in effect, that it is not enough for a man to be a child of Abraham, not enough to keep all the requirements of the Law; this gives him at best the status of a servant in his Father's house. If a man would enter the kingdom of God, he must be born again from above as a child of God, content only to trust and to be sure that he is loved; only thus can he be a child in his Father's house; this is what it means "to see the kingdom of God". We may note in passing that only here in this Gospel does the phrase, "the kingdom of God", occur; an indication, we may think, of an authentic reminiscence of the words actually used.

To this Nicodemus did not say No, but he protested that the impossible was being required of him; "you would destroy the very foundation of my life and of my religious experience; I can't start again; I can no more make a fresh start now than I can re-enter my mother's womb and be born again". To this Jesus replies, in effect, "No, I know you can't, but it might happen to you all the same. The wind blows where it will; you cannot tell whence it comes, nor whither it is going. The movings of the Spirit of God are mysterious like that." If Jesus really spoke of being born of *water* as well as Spirit, the reference must be to the baptism of John, but it is altogether more probable that John II has here interpolated a reference to later Christian baptism. When Nicodemus protests that this is all very difficult, Jesus replies, perhaps with reference to the religion of Abraham and of the prophets, "there is nothing new about this; as a teacher of Israel, you really ought to know this for yourself".

Of the upshot of this conversation we know only that Nicodemus was moved by what Jesus said, that he held him in profound respect, and that later, with Joseph of Arithmathea, he shewed great courage in asking Pilate for leave to dispose decently of the dead body of this Teacher. If, as I suppose, in this passage we have an authentic, though greatly abbreviated, account of a conversation between Jesus and this spiritually-minded Pharisee who came to talk with him, the story is of great historical interest and importance. In the Synoptists we have in general some account of the things Jesus said to the crowds that gathered round him. Here we have a brief note, ultimately, as we may suppose, from Nicodemus himself, of the kind of thing Jesus said in private to an educated man who came in sincerity to consult with him. It may be noted in passing that if I have at all correctly interpreted this conversation, then Paul's great and complicated argument on justification by faith in *Galatians* and in *Romans* is, in substance, close to what Jesus said to Nicodemus, as is his teaching on rebirth through death and resurrection (Rom. VI. 4. Col. II. 12).

Verses 11–21 must be treated as Johannine. In verses 13–21 Jesus is spoken of in the third person; this can be no part of a conversation. Verse 11 begins as if Jesus were speaking, but it passes at once to the testimony of the Church. Jesus might have said something like verse 12 in connection with his parabolic teaching, but here it has no relevance. These verses, then, however great their weight as an expression of the Church's faith, do not serve us in the attempt to find John I behind John II.

III. 22–36. Here again we have a narrative (vv. 22–30) followed by a Johannine commentary. This commentary is really a continuation of verses 11–21, and, unless we suppose some dislocation of the sheets, it is not possible to guess why the story of the Baptist is interpolated here. Verses 31–36 are entirely Johannine and are not to be taken as the Baptist's words.

It is only from John I that we learn that for a time there was a parallel baptism-ministry of John and Jesus. The Baptist at this time was baptising, not in the Jordan but at a place near by called Aenon where there was plenty of water. Jesus was baptising elsewhere in the neighbourhood. Twice we are told that Jesus himself baptised (III. 22 and IV. 1), but this idea was apparently uncongenial to later ecclesiastical thought, and John II (surely it is he!) introduces a little note (IV. 2) to the effect that of course Jesus baptised by proxy only.

If we are concerned with 'Christian baptism', we should note that no distinction is here made between the baptism of Jesus and the baptism of John. But there may just possibly have been some distinction in the stress each laid upon the rite, for we read (v. 25) that the disciples of John had a controversy with 'a Jew' (or, according to some mss, with 'Jews') about purification. Nothing whatever is said about this controversy, and the narrative goes on that John's disciples went to their Master to complain of the greater success of Jesus' mission. The suggestion has been hazarded that 'a Jew' is an alteration of the text from an original which said that there was some controversy between John's followers and Jesus or his followers. Jesus, perhaps we might presume to guess, laid less stress upon the physical aspect of the rite.

To his followers' complaint John replies that a man can only exercise the gifts that God has given him; for himself he had never claimed to be the Chosen One; before this he had pointed to Jesus and now says that his relation to him is like that of the 'best man' to the bridegroom; "he must increase, but I must decrease". We have already seen the profound impression which Jesus made upon John at the time of his baptism, and in view of the astonishing tribute which Jesus is elsewhere reported to have paid to John (Luke VII. 24 ff.) we may accept the picture given here as true to history.

IV. 1–42. The Synoptists say it was the arrest of the Baptist that led Jesus to move north into Galilee; here it is suggested that the move was due to Pharisaic concern at the success of Jesus' mission (IV. 1); the two views are not contradictory. On his way up country Jesus converses with the Samaritan woman at the well. Of this conversation Howard observes* that "the descriptive context supplies a setting for a typical Johannine dialogue. The themes are the living water and a spiritual worship leading to Jesus' self-disclosure as Messiah". This judgement represents, I think, the general view of modern scholarship, nor do I venture to question it except in so far as it presupposes, or is content to take it, that there is no historical basis for the story. It may, of course, be wholly the invention of the evangelist, but in that case we should have to ascribe to him remarkable gifts of novel-writing. It will be

* The Interpreter's Bible ad loc.

much simpler to assume that with a Samaritan woman Jesus had a memorable conversation, which has, no doubt, been rewritten and re-cast in Johannine language.

If this conversation or anything like it took place, John I could only have learnt it either from Jesus himself or from the Samaritan woman. In neither case could we expect a verbally accurate account, but as Thucydides made every effort to ascertain the facts, and then composed speeches to fit the situation, we are at liberty to guess that John I did know in general what Jesus and the woman said. Jesus is reported to have spent two days in Samaria, and I find a possible hint that it was from the woman that John I learnt the story. In our traditional version we read (v. 6) that Jesus "sat thus by the well". What can 'thus' mean here? Neither the modern Revised American version nor, so far as I can see, does *The New English Bible* translate the Greek word for 'thus' at all. Moffatt represents it by "just as he was". This, I suppose, is possible, but is a very curious use of the Greek word. The natural translation would be, "this is how he was sitting by the well", as if the speaker by some gesture indicated what was meant. This could only have been the woman. But I will not lay stress upon a small and doubtful point.

We understand that the disciples, of whom John may well have been one, had gone into the town to get provisions. It was about midday. Jesus, who was very tired, they had left sitting on the famous well of Jacob. A Samaritan woman came out to draw water. I propose to tell the sequel as it might conceivably have been related by the woman herself.* I am frankly guessing, but I claim only, (1) that John II is not likely to have invented this story out of his imagination; (2) that my reconstruction is derived directly from the text; (3) that I offer a perfectly possible or imaginable conversation between Jesus and this woman, and (4) that if any such conversation really took place, it would be represented by John II in the form in which we have it.

"When I came up to the well, there was a Jew sitting there who asked me to give him a drink of water. I was very much astonished because, as you know, Jews will not drink from the same vessels as Samaritans; besides, he must have known that a woman does

---

* I think that in this interpretation I owe much to an essay by the late Canon Bigg which I read very many years ago.

not normally come alone to draw water, least of all at midday; he must have guessed the kind of person I am. I expressed my astonishment, and he looked at me and said: 'If you knew what God would give you, and if you knew what my mission is, you would have asked me, and I would have given you living water.'*
His look made me feel uncomfortable, but I thought I would pass it off as a joke; did he really think he was greater than our father Jacob, and how was he going to get this living water without a bucket? He looked at me again, and said: 'If you once receive the water that I would give you, you would never be thirsty again.' I was getting more and more uncomfortable and tried to shrug it off. 'That would be lovely,' I said; 'I'm tired of coming all this way to fetch water.' He looked at me again, indeed he had never taken his eyes off me, and said: 'Go and call your husband and come back here.' 'I haven't got a husband,' I snapped back at him. How he knew I cannot tell – he must have been a mind-reader – but he told me I had had five husbands and the man I am now living with is not my husband. Naturally I did not want to talk about my private life, so I said to him: 'Sir, I see you are a prophet; you will be interested in religion. Now, you are a Jew, and you Jews say God ought to be worshipped in Jerusalem, and we say on Mount Gerizim; I should very much like to know what you think about that controversy.' But my effort to put him off was useless. 'God can be worshipped in Jerusalem or on Mount Gerizim or anywhere else,' he said; 'worship is not a matter of place but of spirit, for God is Spirit.' Well, of course I could not carry on the discussion on those lines, so I said: 'All that is beyond me; they say that Messiah is coming one day; when he comes, he will explain all that.' He looked at me and said: 'It is I whom God has sent to explain this to you.' Luckily, at that moment his friends came up; I made my escape, and I was in such a hurry to tell people in the village of this extraordinary experience and of this strange person that I actually fled away leaving my precious water-pot behind."

I do not suggest for a moment that I have accurately reported what occurred, but I would put it to readers that, if I have at all correctly interpreted the story, it is much more likely to be a record of a real conversation than a work of literary genius by

* Running water is, in Semitic idiom, living water.

the unknown editor or editors of the Gospel. If I am in any degree right, we have an almost unparalleled indication of the way in which Jesus dealt with an individual who tried to escape from the challenge of his compassionate and piercing word and look.

The disciples on their return were naturally astonished to find Jesus in deep conversation with this woman, and such a woman, but no one ventured to question him about it. This is, possibly, another very slight indication that the story of the conversation comes from the woman herself. There was time for that since, we are told, Jesus and the disciples spent two days in Samaria.

We are not told whether, in fact, the woman had given Jesus a drink of water. We know that he was very tired before she came. After this conversation he was apparently so exhausted that he could not even eat, or, possibly, was so refreshed that he felt no need to eat. "I have bread to eat that you know nothing of." They wondered if he had somehow fed while they were away; no, "My food is to do the will of him that sent me and to accomplish his work." (v. 34).

Jesus had made a profound impression upon this poor woman; she had gone off post-haste to get all her neighbours to come and meet him. Jesus himself, it might seem, was himself deeply moved. He reminded his disciples of the familiar saying: "Four months now, and the harvest will be here"; "Look round about you," he said, "and you will see that the fields are white for the harvest now." (v. 35). We might perhaps have expected John here to quote the reported saying of Jesus: "Pray, therefore, the Lord of the harvest that he may send forth labourers for his harvesting" (Matt. IX. 38. Luke X. 2). Instead of this, we are given another folk-saying: "One sows, another reaps," but of this little section (vv. 36–38) I cannot make good sense in the context. I strongly suspect that the first proverbial saying suggested to the evangelist the second, which is interpreted in terms of an exhortation to the Church in later days when the Gospel was first written.

It would, no doubt, be quite unhistorical to suppose that after this two days' stay the Samaritans recognised Jesus as "the Saviour of the world". This is, so to put it, typical Johannine reporting of which we shall come to many more instances. We should be wise to understand that the Samaritans were deeply moved and began to see that which later became explicit when Jesus was recognised as the Saviour of the world.

IV. 43–54. Verses 43–45 suggest that the reason why Jesus began his ministry with the Baptist in the south is that he realised he would not quickly be accepted in the north, where he was known as the carpenter's son. When he did go north, the Galileans were prepared to listen to him because of the 'signs' he had done and the impression he had made first in Judaea. This may be an accurate historical reminiscence.

Verses 46–54. Jesus' second 'sign' or, as we say, miracle, in Galilee, like the first, was connected with Cana. We might guess that John's informant in both cases was Nathanael, whose home was there. It is likely enough, as commentators suggest, that the story here given is a variant of that narrated in Matthew. VIII. 5–13 and Luke VII. 1–10. That the three accounts vary in detail, and even in more than detail, is no matter for wonder. All three accounts were written down many years after the event, and when there were, no doubt, many traditions of Jesus' healings. The hypothesis upon which I am working makes me tend to think that John II's account is likely to be most accurate, because – although I do not suppose that John I was present – we are, as I suggest, in this Gospel nearest to one who personally knew Jesus. He remembers being told that it was at one p.m. that the official came to plead with Jesus for his boy who was apparently dying. The official, who had heard of Jesus' wonderful cures in Judaea, had no doubt of his ability to heal his son. It rather looks (v. 48) as if the Galileans who heard the request urged him: "Do go; if you succeed in this case, we shall believe the stories we have heard of you in Judaea;" for Jesus rebukes them (plural), as if he said: "Have you no spiritual insight? You will not believe what I say unless you see signs and marvels." Jesus can hardly have said to the anxious father, as our text has it (v. 50), "Your son is alive," which might mean no more than that he is not dead yet. The father clearly understands Jesus to say: "Your son is going to recover"; later, he verifies the fact that the son took a turn for the better, or the crisis passed, at the very moment, one p.m., when Jesus spoke to him.

It is idle, at this distance of time, to seek to explain or explain away Jesus' 'miracles' of healing. In the first place, we have no means of diagnosing the complaint, and in the second we do not know the limits of the power of 'mind' over 'matter'; there are well-attested records in plenty from modern times of healings which baffle the medical profession. In the third place, Jesus was, on any showing, a most extraordinary person; we cannot know by what gifts of clairvoyance – if that be the right term – Jesus knew that the boy would recover. We can accept the story as it stands, without explaining it.

A note will be in place here concerning the use of the word 'believe' in this Gospel; it has already occurred more than once. Here, the official is said to have believed what Jesus said to him (v. 50) and, at the end of the story, "himself believed and his whole house." Earlier, it had been said of the Samaritans: "Now we believe ... and know that this is indeed the Christ, the Saviour of the world" (IV. 42). In the passage now before us (v. 48), Jesus complains that the people will not 'believe' unless they see signs and marvels. There is no doubt what 'to believe' means to the Evangelist. His book was written, he tells us, "that you may believe that Jesus is the Christ, the Son of God, and that believing you may have life through his name" (XX.31). It would be clearly unhistorical to suppose that the Samaritans, or the official and his family could – at this stage – have in this sense 'believed'. Indeed, according to the theology of John II saving faith was only possible after the crucifixion (XVI. 31). But Jesus himself, as the Synoptists make plain, called for belief: 'only believe'. Believe what? The Greek word for 'believe' is of the same root as the word for 'faith'. The nearest English word to represent both verb and noun is 'trust'. Jesus said, in effect: "Trust me, trust what I say, trust in the God of whom I tell you." This is a demand for more than mere intellectual acceptance of certain propositions; it is the requirement of an acceptance with the heart as well as with the mind. It is a call, in W. H. Cadman's happy phrase, for a "trustful persuasion about the truth of the utterance".*
In this sense it is not at all impossible to suppose that under the enormous impression which Jesus made on those who met him, the Samaritans and the officer and his family 'believed'.

* *Studia Evangelica* 1959. p. 432.

Whether their faith held through the dark days to come, we cannot tell.

There does not seem to be any imaginable reason, theological, symbolical or devotional, why John II should have gone out of his way to say that this was the second 'sign' which Jesus did in Galilee, unless, in fact, he had been so told by John I. There is further confirmation of this supposition, if I have rightly interpreted verse 48.

V. 1–47. The story of the sick man at the pool of Bethesda gives a different impression of Jesus' healing ministry from that which we derive from the Synoptic Gospels. We read in *Mark* (I. 32) that after the healing of Peter's mother-in-law at Capernaum 'the whole city' gathered at the door, bringing all the sick and the possessed, and Jesus healed many of them. This may be taken to imply that he did not cure all of them. So *Luke* says (IV. 40.f.) that he laid his hands upon all that were brought to him and tended them, in many cases casting out evil spirits or, if we wish to put it in this way, that some he failed to heal. Only *Matthew* (VIII. 16) says that he healed *all* who were brought to him. In general, however, we derive from the Synoptists an impression both of mass healings and of a demand for faith on the part of the person healed. This may not be a wholly false impression, but it may be contrasted with the story before us, which carries with it the mark of authenticity and, presumably, the testimony of an eye-witness of what happened.

It would appear that John I accompanied Jesus in Judaea rather than in Galilee. We are back in Jerusalem. It is presumably early in the ministry of Jesus, for he is not yet a well-known figure (v. 13). He comes to the pool of Bethesda, the ruins of which, as I gather, are still to be seen below the basilica of St Anne. This was a famous place for miraculous cures.* It seems that no one recognises Jesus there, or at least none appeals to him for help. He feels moved of himself to approach and address one single invalid. Here we can only say, I think, that Jesus had an extraordinary power (which others have shared in lesser degree) of reading a

* vv. 3–4. are almost certainly a later insertion into the text to explain v. 7. *v.* Barrett, *The Gospel according to St. John, ad loc.*

man's character and life-history from his face. The earlier story
of Nathanael was a further illustration of this power. In the
present case we are justified in assuming (from v. 14) that Jesus
diagnosed this particular man's infirmity as what the doctors call
'hysterical'; its cause was mental, not organic. Jesus goes up to
this man and asks him whether he really wants to be cured; the
man says: "Of course I do, but I never have the chance of getting
first into the water when it is stirred, which is the only hope of
being cured." Jesus says to him: "Get up; pick up your mattress
and walk." The man obeys and finds he can. Jesus slips away, and
the man has no idea who his benefactor is. Later, Jesus comes across
the man in the Temple and says to him: "Look, you are well now;
do not go on sinning, lest something worse befall you." Just what
Jesus had in mind we cannot tell, for we do not know the man
who had been healed.

The Gospels often tell us what Jesus said, but only rarely speak
of how he looked. We therefore think of him pre-eminently as a
teacher. It was said of Luther that "his eyes sparkle and glitter like
a star, so that it is hardly possible to look at them". We should not
wish so to speak of the eyes of Jesus; but when he looked into a
man's face, he read him through and through, and when he
caught the man's eye, his look had a compelling force. If anyone
else had said to this sick man "get up and walk", he would have
thought he was being mocked. When Jesus looked into his eyes
and said these words, he was able to obey. This is not a question of
'miracle' in the old-fashioned sense; it is a measure of the stature of
this prophet out of Galilee.

All this happened on the Sabbath. When the man was seen
carrying his mattress, the authorities told him that he was breaking
the Law by doing this. The man answered, in effect: "I don't
know anything about that; all I know is that the man who healed
me told me to do this." When, later, he found out who Jesus was,
he gave his name to the authorities. That, we read (v. 16), is why
the authorities began to look out for Jesus (the imperfect tense is
important here) to stop this kind of thing.

The story, so far, seems to carry its authenticity upon its face,
but it is followed (vv. 17–47) by a long discourse in the now
familiar Johannine style and language which cannot be taken as an
authentic account of what Jesus actually said. It is likely enough,

however, that the authorities, having learnt Jesus' name, should seek him out and challenge what he had presumed to do. John I may quite well have been present at this interview. I read this discourse not as the pure imaginative invention of John II, but as the translation of the substance of Jesus' actual reply, set down and elaborated in the language and thought-forms of a later Christian generation. For instance, as Dr Caird has suggested to me, verses 19 and 20, may well be taken from some parable of Jesus drawn from his own experience when in the carpenter's shop in Nazareth he watched and copied Joseph.

First, then, I should rule out verses 20–29 as plainly Christian meditation; they express the Church's faith, but do not answer the question put to Jesus. I think that Jesus said to the authorities something like this: "God's works of mercy are unceasing; they do not pause on the Sabbath day; we, therefore, are called to works of mercy likewise on every day" (v. 17). Even if, in fact, Jesus said 'I', not 'we', must do the works of mercy every day, he was not thereby "making himself equal with God", nor should we suppose that at this early stage the authorities were determined to kill him, though no doubt they wanted to stop him. Verse 18, therefore, I regard as an editorial gloss. "When I saw that poor man there," I conceive Jesus as saying further, "it was as if I heard what God would say to him and would now do for him, and I simply acted in God's name" (v. 19).

"But what authority have you to act like that?" asked the authorities.

"I make no claims for myself," answered Jesus; "I am simply seeking to do the will of him who sent me, for I am sure that God sent me (v. 30). If I made claims for myself, there is no reason why you should accept them; my only authentication comes from God himself (vv. 31 f.). Take the case of John the Baptist. He was a burning and a shining lamp, and while he was allowed to minister, you could recognise that. I am conscious of a further ministry, and its authentication is what God does through me (vv. 33–36). No human ear has ever heard God; we have to walk by faith, accepting the testimony of those who seem to have been sent to us by him (vv. 37 f.). Or consider the Scriptures. Can you deny that they support what I am saying and doing? (v. 39). I make no claims for myself, but if you have the love of God in your hearts, you will recognise my calling (vv. 40.f.). If anyone appears claiming to be a prophet or the Promised One, you give serious attention to his claims; you cannot repudiate what I am saying and doing simply because I make no personal claims (v. 43). I can understand your position well enough; it is Moses, not I, who reproaches you. If you did not misunderstand Moses, you would recognise that implicit in his teaching is that which I am teaching and doing now" (vv. 45–47).

I pause to comment. No one will deny that this is what Jesus might have said when his authority was challenged, but if I am justified in my assumption that John II did not invent, but translated into his own later theological terms, the reminiscences of John I, we may claim that, in all probability, this is – in substance – what Jesus did actually say to those who challenged him. This is a picture of Jesus, compatible with, but quite distinct from, the picture we derive from the Synoptic Gospels, which were concerned to pass on such of his teaching as would be of service to the Church of their day, and were little concerned with giving an historical picture of how Jesus dealt with individuals and what he said to those who challenged his authority. Moreover, while John II in his Gospel represents Jesus as making all manner of claims: "I am the Bread of Life", "I am the Good Shepherd", "I am the Vine", "I am the Resurrection and the Life", the picture of the historic Jesus as depicted by John I is of one who made no claims whatever for himself, but simply called men to recognise the voice and hand of God in what he said and did.

VI. 1–15. The feeding of the five thousand, taken as a miracle, raises the profoundest doubts in our minds. Even if we are not prepared to dogmatise about what is possible and what is not, a marvel of this kind seems to us quite out of character. Earlier generations had no difficulty in believing the narrative as it stands; we cannot thus uncritically accept it. But the story recurs in all the Synoptists (Mark VI. 31–44; Matt. XIV. 13–21; Luke IX. 10–17) and, indeed, if we may take "the feeding of the four thousand" (Mark VIII. 1–19; Matt. XV. 32–39) as a doublet, we may say that we have no less than six accounts of this strange meal. It is possible to surmise from the Synoptists that it marked a crisis or turning-point in the ministry of Jesus, but this is only made explicit in this Gospel.

We cannot know whether John himself was there, but since he tells us what Philip said and what Andrew said, we may suppose that perhaps he was there himself. Dr Barrett, may, of course, be right that the mention of names is a mark of 'lateness'.* It is, however, as legitimate to regard it as the eye-witness's recollection. What can we make of the 'miracle'? Very little; we can only guess. I should have antecedently supposed it likely that crowds coming from a considerable distance for a meeting that would not be short would have brought some provisions with them. We are at liberty to suppose, if we like, that Jesus suggested a pooling of resources; all he and his companions could offer was five loaves and two fish which they, presumably, bought from the boy who was carrying them. Jesus made the people sit down; he then took the loaves with a prayer of thanksgiving (saying eucharist over them, to borrow the Greek word). The meal was then shared, and everyone was satisfied. That John, if he was present, alleged that, when the meal was over, they filled twelve basketfuls of the remains of the five loaves is not to be believed. This is an element from the legend intended to heighten the miracle and was, perhaps, inserted here by John II because it was a familiar piece of the tradition as the Synoptists also have reported it.

The 'miracle' obscures the significance of the event. Jesus' popularity, as we may suppose, was at its height. The people said of him: "this is he for whom we have been looking, he who can lead us into the new age of God which he proclaims"; but, to most of them, this will have implied: "let him lead us against the hated Romans". Here indeed was a critical situation for the ministry of Jesus. If this cry were taken up, as well it might be in these tumultuous days, not only would the authorities at once intervene, but Jesus' real message and significance would be completely falsified. The reader will find a vivid portrayal of the intense fanaticism of the times in the chapter entitled "the Ivory Gate" of Lionel Curtis' *Civitas Dei* (Bk. 1). Jesus managed to slip away from his admirers, perhaps as darkness came on, and retired alone into the mountains, partly, no doubt, to escape from a popular demonstration, but also that he might have

* op. cit. p. 228.

solitude for prayer in which to face this new and dangerous situation.

VI. 16–25. This miraculous story, as told in the Gospel, is followed by a double miracle. Jesus, it would seem, had instructed his close companions to leave him alone and make their way to Capernaum by boat. It was late and dark; they got caught in a storm, and we are then to understand, first, that when they had rowed three or four miles from the shore, they saw Jesus walking on the water in the middle of the lake, and, second, that when they wanted to take him on board they suddenly found themselves in the harbour at Capernaum. (v. 21). What really happened? We cannot tell. Howard, in his commentary on this Gospel, writes:* "In Mark (VI. 45–56) the disciples are making for Bethsaida, and the impression left upon a modern reader is that they were coasting along by the shore and were nearing the head of the lake when a strong northerly wind drove them back to a place not far from where they had left Jesus. Here they took Jesus on board, and finally landed in the district of Gennesaret, not far from Capernaum." We may note that the words usually translated "walking on the sea" might legitimately be translated "walking by the seaside", for that is clearly their meaning when they recur in John XXI. 1.

If John I himself narrated this event, we can only guess what he may have said. As in the cases of the turning of the water into wine at Cana and the feeding of the 'five thousand' on the mountain, legendary elements – very impressive to pre-scientific generations – have been inserted to heighten the wonder. It is, perhaps, legitimate to surmise that setting off at dusk the disciples got caught in a storm when darkness fell. When they had rowed a very long way, as it seemed to them, though in fact they had been blown back almost to their starting point, they suddenly saw Jesus walking, as they supposed, upon the waters of the lake. They were, very naturally, extremely scared. Jesus calmed them, assuring them that it really was himself, and not an apparition. They wanted then to take him on board and discovered that, as a matter of fact, they had come back to land. The experience was alarming

* *The Interpreter's Bible,* ad loc.

enough, and legend quickly grows. But, as I have said, how much of the narrative goes back to the supposed eye-witness we cannot determine now.

Even if five thousand be taken as a round figure, or an exaggerated guess, we should hardly suppose that a very considerable crowd bivouacked on the hillside through that stormy night. But some, at least, seem to have stayed in the vicinity. Next morning they were puzzled. Jesus was nowhere to be seen; there had been only one boat on the previous night, and Jesus' companions had been seen to row off in that. Luckily for them, however, they were able to hail some boats (blown off their course by the storm, perhaps) and get a lift – certainly not five thousand! – back to Capernaum. When they came to Capernaum, they found Jesus, and asked him how he had got there.

VI. 26–71. This long passage purports to be a discourse by Jesus, occasionally interrupted by questions, the main theme of which is himself as the Bread of Life. The whole passage is Johannine in style and language, nor can we doubt that in composing it the evangelist has the Christian eucharist in mind. The discourse opens as if it were addressed to those who asked Jesus how he had got back to Capernaum, but later we gather that it was spoken in the synagogue at Capernaum (v. 59). It is a great theological disquisition which cannot be taken as historical in the form in which we have it. John II had no historic sense, as we understand the term; he makes no clear distinction between what Jesus said on earth and what he was now saying to the believing Church; it was the same Jesus, the same message. Nonetheless, John II did not consciously invent; he always supposed he was narrating what really happened (XX. 30 f. XXI. 24 f.).

It may, I think, be possible by an exercise of historic imagination with some degree of confidence to guess the facts underlining this highly artificial and manifestly theological discourse. My attempted reconstruction rests upon three suppositions. First, it is legitimate to suggest that at the memorable meal on the hill-side Jesus may have said, in effect: "We haven't much food here for this big company, but the needs of the body are secondary to the needs of the soul, and I shall speak to you about the bread which comes down from heaven." He will, so to put it, have taken for his text his earlier word to his disciples: "my food is to do the will of him that sent me". Second, I suppose that he spoke of the coming Kingdom and the national destiny in such moving and glowing terms that the audience, being carried away and far from deeply understanding his meaning, thought to 'make him king' or to come forward as the new leader of the nation. Third, I suppose that the meeting on the hill-side, however it ended, was indecisive; Jesus slipped away, perhaps as darkness fell; but the issue could not be left where it was. Therefore, on the following Sabbath, there being no danger of popular demonstrations on that day, he went to the synagogue to make his meaning as plain as possible. These suppositions are guesses, but they are legitimate, and if they be provisionally accepted they afford an historic background for the address which John II has elaborated in his own peculiar fashion.

Jesus' hearers in the synagogue may be supposed to say to him, "you speak about doing the works of God, but you will not lead us against the Romans; then what are we to do that we may work the works of God?" (v. 28). Jesus replies (v. 29), "this is the work that God requires: believe in the one whom he has sent". The reply was not paradoxical; it was shattering. Here was an audience full of enthusiastic hopes, longing for national deliverance, ready to do anything, to give life itself, if their religious aspirations might thereby be fulfilled. We may imagine the drop in the temperature when, instead of some call to arms, Jesus says to them, in effect, "God only requires one thing of you, that you trust me, that you believe that God has sent me and commit yourselves to God and follow me".

When Jesus had replied, "the only thing that God requires of you to do is to trust me", it would be natural and inevitable that there should be the further question, "Yes, but if we trust you, what is it you would have us do?" Jesus' answer, in briefest form might be paraphrased at length: "You are anxious, you are puzzled, you are frustrated; you are looking for the new age of God, and nothing happens; you are hungry for the bread of life; you are losing hope; you are walking in darkness. He that follows me shall not walk in darkness any more; his hunger shall be stayed. In other words, what you are to do is to follow me."

The Fourth Gospel never makes plain what 'following' him will mean. Many scholars have supposed that John II had read Mark's Gospel, but it is entirely possible that he had read none of our Synoptic Gospels,* but he will certainly have known, as his readers will certainly have known, the general – perhaps still only oral – tradition of the teaching of Jesus. To glimpse the glory of God in the lilies of the field, to mark his indiscriminate mercy in the sending of the former and the latter rain, to live a life of compassion for all in need of succour, to love their enemies – that was to follow Jesus, and those who so followed him would feed upon the bread of life, though the decisive act of God in the inauguration of the new age was not seen yet. We misread the Fourth Gospel unless we see that it presupposes, not indeed our Synoptic Gospels, but a knowledge of what Jesus taught in word and deed.

Howard in his commentary† says, "there was a rabbinical rule that if a prophet who was not yet recognised as such should give a sign or wonder, he must be listened to; otherwise no heed need be given to him". "You claim to speak to us with a prophet's authority," the people are represented as saying to him; "then give us a sign like, for instance, the manna which certified the calling of Moses, as Scripture says, 'he gave them bread from heaven'. You speak of the heavenly bread; well, show it to us, let us see it." Jesus is reported to have answered, "I am the bread of life; he that comes to me shall never hunger, and he that believes on me shall never thirst" (v. 35).

We, who through the Synoptists have seen the kind of way in which Jesus spoke and the necessity of preserving 'the Messianic secret', do not believe that he ever said in public "I am the bread of life". We tend, therefore, to reject this passage as Johannine theology. Yet, if we come to think of it, this is precisely, in substance, what he must have said. Much has been written by the learned about "the self-consciousness of Jesus". I should be at a loss to describe the self-consciousness of my close friends or even my own self-consciousness. How much more in respect of the self-consciousness of Jesus are we out of our depth: "Sir, thou hast nothing to draw with, and the well is deep." But certain

* *v* Gardner-Smith. *St. John and the Synoptic Gospels.*
† *The Interpreter's Bible,* ad. vv. 30 ff.

inferences we may safely make. The ministry of Jesus overlapped
for a while with that of John the Baptist, but Jesus clearly knew
himself called to a ministry beyond that of John. He proclaimed,
with the Baptist, the imminence of the decisive act of God, but
he was called, not to declare the vengeance of God, but "to
proclaim release to the captives and recovering of sight to the
blind, and to set at liberty them that are oppressed" (Luke IV. 18).
His calling was vindicated by his mighty works: "if I by the finger
of God cast out demons, without doubt God's kingdom is come
upon you" (Luke XI. 20). This message and mission was given to
him and to him alone. He was the Messenger, the Witness, the
Son. He could see, for even we can see, that the destiny of his
nation depended upon whether or not it would accept his message; for individuals it was a matter of life or death, spiritual life
or spiritual death, whether they accepted him or not. He knew
that he had been sent not merely to speak, like a prophet, but to
act in the name of God. It was impossible to distinguish himself
from his message and his action. He *was*, and he must have known
that he was, the bread of life to men. It is in the highest degree
unlikely that he ever said, "I am the bread of life", but that is
precisely, though not verbally, what he was bound to say. He is
here, no doubt, misquoted but not misrepresented.

It is easy to believe that if Jesus made these claims for himself,
even implicitly, there should have been protests (vv. 41–50): "Isn't
this just Jesus, Joseph's son, whose father and mother we know?
Who is he to claim a heavenly calling or to offer us what he calls
the bread from heaven, as if in the Law we did not already possess
this bread, and as if we were not all Abraham's children and heirs
of salvation?" (vv. 41 f.). Speaking like the prophets of old in the
name of God, Jesus may well have said something like this (vv.
44 ff.): "I know that I was sent by God to declare to you that the
kingdom of God is now at hand; the bread of life is God's Kingdom in your hearts. The Kingdom is open to everyone, for does
not Scripture itself say, 'they shall every one of them be taught of
God'? The entry into it is not by descent from Abraham, but by
personal obedience and faith. To you, to all, I bring the bread of
life which is God's gift to you. Accept God's sending of me, and
enter the Kingdom now."

The Synoptic narratives represent Jesus as the Teacher, the

heavenly Wisdom, the great Healer. In the reminiscences of John I
we see him as the ineluctable evangelist and realise that it was a
terrible thing for any but the very few to meet with him. To say
'Yes' to him was to be committed to a life unknown, unpredictable
and perilous; to say 'No' to him was to have glimpsed the glory
of God and chosen darkness. No man could ever be the same again
having met with him. We can read the other Gospels overlooking
the tension Jesus set up in the hearts of men. Is he mad, or is this
indeed God's word to us? Jesus was the divine evangelist, and
from the nature of the case his own evangel. Such was the power
and such the stature of this man!

In verse 51 Jesus is said to identify his flesh with the heavenly
bread. Hearers protest, "how can this man give us his flesh to eat"?;
they are told that they must eat his flesh and drink his blood (vv.
51–58). It is not useful for our purpose to enter into speculations
as to the processes of thought whereby in this Graeco-Roman
world there could have arisen from any imaginable saying of
Jesus a doctrine that in the Christian eucharist his flesh is eaten and
his blood drunk. It is inconceivable that Jesus, or John I, or any
Hebrew could ever have spoken of eating the flesh and drinking
the blood of the Christ; for the idea of drinking blood was utterly
repulsive to the Hebrew mind, and any metaphor from canni-
balism, however remote, is unimaginable to it.

That this conclusion of the sermon is Johannine and not of
John I is, perhaps, indicated by the suggestion that the controversy
these words aroused took place after the meeting in the synagogue
(v. 60). The protest or objection is met in two ways: first, the
questioners are told that this is no greater wonder than that which
they are one day to see, namely, the Ascent of Jesus into heaven,
and, second, it is explained – but very obscurely – that somehow
this doctrine is to be spiritually, not literally, interpreted. This is
not history but Church doctrine in the making.

On the other hand, we can well believe that in the synagogue
at Capernaum on this Sabbath morning Jesus did, in fact, say
that about his mission and purpose which caused great offence
and, as we are here told (v. 66), lost him the greater part of his
following. He has explained to them that the heavenly bread, the
bread of life, is not theirs as descended from Abraham but only as
it is accepted personally by obedience and faith; he has made it

101

clear that the nation is called to a spiritual, not a political, revolution, "and from that time on many of those who had followed him retired and went about with him no more" (v. 66). Indeed the crowd, at least for the time being, deserted him. He turns to the inner circle of his followers and asks, "are you going to leave me too?" (v. 67). Simon Peter answers for the others and says, in effect, "we are puzzled also, but we shall stand by you, for, though we cannot understand, yet what you say to us comes home to us as the word of life" (v. 68). Whether Peter went on to say, in these words, "we have believed that you are the Holy One of God" we cannot know; in *Mark* I. 24 and *Luke* IV. 34 this title is put into the mouth of a demoniac. But Peter may well have said, in some words, "we are convinced that God has sent you" (v. 69).

It is difficult to believe that at this stage Jesus so foresaw the future course of events, that he knew that Judas of Kerioth was going to betray him (v. 70), but he may well have said, in effect, "I have chosen you to be my close disciples, but even now you do not understand what this will involve for you". He was comforted by their response, but knew them better than they knew themselves.

This chapter is properly regarded as a great statement of Johannine theology. Treat it, however, not indeed as history but as based on history, and it reveals the towering spiritual stature of the prophet out of Galilee. Jesus has first made the crowd forget their hunger and then so moved them by his words that they are ready to recognise in him the one that should lead their nation into the promised and eagerly expected new age of God. Then, deliberately, on the following Sabbath, abating no claim, he refuses to offer any 'proof' of his calling, explains that the revolution of the new age is spiritual, not political, that the heavenly food is to do the Father's will, and that to do his will is to accept his own call and mission. He is teacher only as evangelist. The majority rejects him.

VII. 1–36. This passage apparently refers to Jesus' next visit to Jerusalem after the healing of the sick man of Bethesda. The narrative is told in Johannine terms, but it seems to me quite arbitrary to suggest that it represents controversies between Christians and Jews towards the end of the first century. Would such controversies have been of much interest to John II's readers? Would they have served the acknowledged purpose of his Gospel? It is, rather, as if we could overhear John I saying, "how well I remember the excitement at that Feast of Tabernacles when Jesus did not appear at first, and everyone was wondering whether he would turn up". For here we have the context, the feel, the atmosphere of the situation at the time.

Vv. 1–13. It may well be that Jesus was exercising his ministry but now, inevitably, in quiet ways in Galilee, for he had heard rumour that in Judaea he was in danger of assassination (vv. 3 f.). The Feast of Tabernacles was now at hand. Jesus' brothers, who do not believe in his mission, say to him, "we are going up to the feast; come with us; this half-secret way of yours is useless; if you really have something to say, come and say it openly to the world". Jesus replies, "it is all very well for you to go up to the feast, but I am not coming with you; you are not in any danger". His brothers, therefore, went off without him. According to the best mss. authority, Jesus said simply, "I am not going". The variant reading "not yet" is probably an alteration to bring this verse into harmony with v. 10. Jesus may have changed his mind. He was missed, and there was much whispering about him, not open discussion for fear of the authorities. Some said, "he is a good man"; others said, "he is a charlatan".

Vv. 14–36. Jesus made a secret journey to Jerusalem and did not appear until the festival was half-way through. When he arrived, he began to teach like a rabbi. Even the Sanhedrin was astonished at the way he dealt with Scripture, but they protested that he lacked all authority. Jesus answers them, in effect, "I have no human authority for what I am teaching; I speak as God puts his word into my mouth; if you are seeking to know and to do God's will, you will be able to judge whether or not I am speaking with divine authority (vv. 16–18). You accuse me of breaking Moses's law by healing on the Sabbath day. Do you yourselves keep the law of Moses?" (Could Paul possibly have been in the crowd when he said that?) "Is my healing on the Sabbath a reason why you should kill me?" "You're mad," they said, "who's talking of killing you?" (v. 20). "The law of Moses," Jesus argues, "demands that a child be circumcised on the eighth day, and you obey this command even if the eighth day happens to be the Sabbath. How can it possibly be right to circumcise a child on the Sabbath and wrong to cure a sick man on the Sabbath?" (vv. 22–24).

To this there was, of course, no answer, and once again we overhear the whispering of the crowd: "this is the man they talked of killing, and here he is, teaching openly, and no one answers him." "Do you suppose the Sanhedrin really suspects that after all he may be the Messiah?" "We certainly don't think so." "The Messiah, as we all know, will come mysteriously, and we know very well where Jesus comes from" (vv. 25–27). If we may judge by silence, John I shows no knowledge of the tradition that Jesus was born in Bethlehem, nor does he anywhere suggest that Joseph was not his father. Gardner-Smith writes of the author of this Gospel, "it is certainly surprising that though he is clearly aware of Jewish objections to the claims of Jesus founded upon a knowledge of his birth and origin, and he twice calls Jesus 'the son of Joseph', he never answers these objections by denying that Joseph was the father of Jesus or by asserting that Jesus was born at Bethlehem. Nor does he ever call Jesus 'the son of David'. The most obvious explanation is that the Fourth Evangelist wrote at a time and in a circle in which the tradition that Jesus was born of the Virgin Mary at Bethlehem, the city of David, had not yet become established. If so, he did not know our Synoptic Gospels".*

These rumours and this talk are brought to the ears of Jesus. When he next appears in the temple he says, in effect, "of course you know who I am and where I come from, just as your fathers knew the prophets and where they came from, but like the prophets it is God's word I speak, not my own, and I know well that he sent me. If you knew God, as you claim to do, you would recognise his voice" (vv. 28 f.). There were cries from the crowd calling for his arrest, but no one laid hands on him. That was to come later. Some of those who heard him, however, were impressed and moved. "Will the Messiah, when he comes," they said, "show more manifest signs of God's presence with him?" (vv. 30 f.). All this excitement and this talk was reported to the Chief Priests who sent their officers to arrest Jesus, who then uttered a very cryptic saying, something like this: "I have only a little time left

* *St. John And The Synoptic Gospels*, p. 39.

104

with you; you will look for me but will not find me; I am going beyond your reach" (v. 33). What did he mean by this, the people asked. Did he mean he was going to appeal to the Greek-speaking Jews of the Diaspora? (vv. 35 f.). Jesus was, presumably, gone when the police arrived, unless, in fact, it was on the last day of the feast that the Sanhedrin sent to arrest him (v. 45), and the notice is here misplaced.

Such a reconstruction is very hazardous and uncertain. In detail it is, no doubt, inaccurate; but I derive it directly from this Gospel; some such scene as this may very well have occurred. John II and his readers were no longer interested in what the crowd muttered in Jerusalem some sixty years ago; it is, therefore, more likely that John II derived it ultimately from John I and told it in his own way. If, in any degree, I am right, we have the kind of direct, local, intimate picture of what happened such as we can hardly ever derive from the Synoptic Gospels. These more accurately represent Jesus' words when they report them, but the historical setting we better derive, though at second-hand and much edited, from John II.

VII. 37-52. It is always open to us to suppose that the Johannine editor was not merely a theologian but was also gifted with the dramatic powers of the novelist; further, it is possible that, though he was presumably a Greek writing for Greeks, he knew that at the Feast of Tabernacles water was brought from Shiloah and poured before the altar in Jerusalem; the heavenly gift of water in the wilderness was thus recalled (Ex. XVII. 6), and there was recited from Isaiah the words, "therefore with joy shall ye draw water out of the wells of salvation" (Is. XII. 3). The narrative in these verses may be a purely literary invention. It appears to me altogether more probable that the editor here rests upon the reminiscences of John I, which he reproduces in his own style and idiom.

On the last day of the feast, then, Jesus appears before the people and declares, "if any man is athirst, let him come to me and drink". This, I conceive, is precisely what he did say, though probably not in just these words. The editor has added a theological comment, which seems plainly to be in error; he says that

Jesus was really referring to the gift of the Spirit which was to come at Pentecost. If I may insert a word into the text, Jesus says, "if any man is athirst, let him come to me *now* and drink." Given the situation, we may, with confidence, say not that Jesus may have said, but that he must have said, something like this. It would be entirely natural that on this day he should speak to the people about the mysterious gift of water under Moses in the wilderness; this, in a sense, was water from heaven, but not the spiritual water which quenches the soul's thirst; that spiritual water is an utter faith and confidence in the heavenly Father; the water in the wilderness was but a type of that which was to come; now the kingdom of God is at hand; it is here; "only trust me that God is speaking through me, and enter into the kingdom, receive the living water; I am offering it to you now." What is this but to say: "If any man thirst, let him come unto me and drink; I am the water of life"? In substance, this is what Jesus must have said, for this was the message he came to bring.

There is this important distinction between him and the prophets who preceded him; they were called in the name of the Lord to *speak* to the people: "thus saith the Lord"; Jesus knew himself called not merely to speak but to act, to declare that the kingdom was at hand and to demonstrate it by his actions in life and death. He was sent to *bring* the kingdom, and however little he may have made claims on his own behalf, he was compelled by his message and calling to say to the people, in effect, "if any man thirst, let him come unto me and drink". The Synoptists give us facts, but in the Fourth Gospel we see both Jesus and the impression he made upon those who heard him. We can even overhear the crowd, some saying, "this man is really a prophet", others, "this must be the Messiah himself", and others replying, "that can't be; we all know that Messiah does not come from Galilee" (vv. 40–42). He was, naturally, in danger of arrest. It would seem that the police arrived and did nothing, and when they were asked by the Sanhedrin why they had not brought him in, they seem to have said, in effect (v. 46), "but we couldn't. We thought you were sending us to arrest a trouble-maker, but when we heard him speak (what he said was beautiful), there was no possible ground for taking him up." "Have you lost your heads too?" asked the angry authorities, "It is we who know best." But even among the authorities there was not complete unanimity, for Nicodemus courageously ventured to suggest that they ought to hear Jesus for themselves before condemning him. His colleagues were very angry; "are you another of these Galileans?" they said, "don't you know that no prophet ever comes out of Galilee?" I have retold the story in my own colloquial terms; let the reader decide whether this is not much more likely to be history than fiction.

VII. 53–VIII. 11. It is almost universally recognised among scholars that the story of the woman taken in adultery (VII. 53–VIII. 11) is no part of the original text of the Fourth Gospel, but none, I suppose, would wish to deny that we have here the record of an event that actually happened. I shall treat it, therefore, as a reminiscence of John I which was very appropriately added after the first publication of the Gospel, a narrative uninfluenced by the theology of John II.

There is brought before Jesus a woman taken in adultery, and he says to her accusers, "let him that is without sin among you cast the first stone". We are apt so to read the story as to miss its gravity.

Whether the woman was, in the primary sense, the guilty party we cannot know, but at least she has been caught in the act, and they have got her. What are they to do with her? Moses prescribed death by stoning, but capital punishment was forbidden the Jews by the Romans, and there will be trouble if they take the law into their own hands. Someone has the happy idea, "let us take her to this Galilean rabbi, and see what he says; he will be contradicting his own teaching if he tells us to stone her, and if he does not, we shall have proved him to disregard the Law. We've got her, and we'll get him too".

I will permit myself at this point an excursion into fantasy. Let us suppose that Jesus was just a very gentle, very kind and very wise man, as many people picture him. I imagine these men bringing the woman before him. "Moses said she is to be stoned; what do you say, rabbi?" The gentle and wise and kind man would perhaps answer, "well, it is true Moses said that, but, after all, you know your own hearts, and you will hardly feel that you are the right people to execute his sentence". "Yes, rabbi, we're none of

107

us perfect; we know that, but, after all, we caught her in the very act, and you know what Moses said; what do you think should be done with her?" I can imagine a very unsatisfactory and inconclusive discussion; and in the end, I suppose, they would have dragged the woman away. What they would have done with her I do not know, but they would have left the gentle and kind and wise rabbi utterly discomfited. I have told this imaginary story in order to make sharp its contrast with what actually happened.

It was a horrible scene; there was the woman's terror and agony; I should not like to have looked on the faces of those men, and it even appears that for a time even Jesus could not look at them. He stooped down and wrote, or seemed to be writing, on the ground. T. W. Manson has suggested that Jesus after the manner of a Roman judge first wrote and then delivered verbally his decision. "Come on, rabbi, tell us what *you* say" (v. 7). At last he looked up, and I conceive that his eye took them all in, none could escape his look. Then he said, "let him that is without sin among you cast the first stone", – *and they slunk out*, one by one.

We do not wonder that another writer could say of him, "his eyes were like a flame of fire, and his voice like the roaring of the sea, and out of his mouth came a two-edged sword, and his face was like the sun shining in the noonday, and when I saw him, I fell at his feet like a dead man" (Rev. I. 14–17). If we can picture those men slinking away at his look and his word, we have a picture of the splendour and the majesty of Jesus.

Jesus is left with the woman standing there alone. Again he bends his eyes to the ground. What is the woman thinking? At last he looks up. "Where are all those who accused you, has no one condemned you?" "No one, sir." "Neither do I condemn you," said Jesus, "you have learnt your lesson."

We may be thankful for the factual objectivity of the Synoptists, but here we have the very picture of Jesus and of the overwhelming impression of his personality.

VIII. 12–20. In this section Jesus appears as the light of the world. The Fourth Gospel gives the impression that Jesus openly and deliberately called attention to himself: "I am the bread of life; let the thirsty come to me; I am the light of the world". In view of the Synoptic Gospels we must rule out such a picture as un-historical, and we may rightly observe that the heavenly bread, the water from heaven, the heavenly light, are key-words of the Johannine theology. It will not follow from this, however, that the conversation or controversy in these verses bears no relation to history and is a theological invention of the editor who, like Plato before him, expounds his philosophy in the form of dia-logue. There seems no conceivable reason why John II should have put in a note to say that the discussion he has recorded took place in or near the treasury unless, in his own way, he were recording that which John I had told him. The Greek word properly means the strongroom; no meetings could take place there. We may perhaps assume, then, that John I was referring to one of the places where money-offerings were received. Ad-mitting, then, that this passage is thoroughly Johannine, and that the discussion cannot have taken place as here reported, we are left with the difficult question what can have been the incident or discussion which the editor, translating it into his own terms, could have rendered in this way.

Here we can only guess, but in so far as we are by now familiar with the Johannine style, and in so far as we may have an undis-torted picture of Jesus, a sober and rational guess should not be beyond us.

We read that in the synagogue at Nazareth Jesus took the scroll, read the passage in Isaiah beginning, "the Spirit of the Lord is upon me ...", and said, "this Scripture is fulfilled before you today". It is entirely possible and likely that on some other occa-sion when he happened to be teaching by the treasury he quoted the passage from Isaiah (IX. 2), "upon the people that sat in dark-ness has a great light shined", and then said, in effect, "this prophecy is fulfilled before you today. The past years have been days of darkness and confusion; we could say of God that 'clouds and darkness are round about him', but now, believe me, the kingdom of God is upon you; the doors are thrown open; God is revealing himself as the Father and Deliverer; the darkness of the night is being scattered by the sun's morning rays; whoever will follow me and trust in my words will no longer be walking in

109

darkness but will possess the light of life". Such was clearly the message and mission of Jesus. The editor is not misrepresenting what Jesus said, except verbally, when he quotes him as saying, "I am the light of the world", for that is precisely the same message in other terms.

There is no improbability, therefore, in supposing that on some memorable occasion, memorable because of the controversy which it provoked, Jesus spoke of the heavenly light, or the light of life, which he was bringing to men. The controversy is re-recorded, of course, in Johannine terminology, but I will venture to paraphrase its course in terms that are historically both intelligible and even probable.

Jesus, I am assuming, has been speaking of the heavenly light, the light of life, the true spiritual light of men, and has declared that any one who follows him, accepting his word and living by it, will not walk in darkness but will have the light of life (v. 12). The representatives of the authorities protest: "that is what you say, but why should we accept your word for it? Who are you, and who gave you authority, to speak like this?" (v. 13). Jesus replies, in effect, "I know that what I say is true; I am as conscious and certain of my divine calling and of this word given me to say, as were ever the prophets before me certain of their mission. You are simply judging by outward appearances, and think I can be no true prophet because I come from Galilee. Moreover, I am not asking you just to take my word for what I am saying; my message is being verified by God himself for, see, it is by the finger of God that I cast out evil spirits; it is not I alone, then, that am bearing this witness; it is being corroborated by my heavenly Father" (vv. 14–18). "We do not recognise this heavenly Father of yours," reply his opponents. To this Jesus answers, in effect, "you are spiritually blind in that you cannot recognise me as sent by God; you have not understood your own religious heritage" There was more talk of having him arrested, but the time had not yet come (v. 20).

All I venture to suggest is that such a scene as I have depicted may very well have been enacted by the treasury in Jerusalem, and that if such a controversy took place our Biblical text (VIII. 12–20) is the way it would have been recorded by the Johannine editor. We may rightly say in our commentaries that Bread and

Water and Light are key-words of the Johannine theology, but that would not mean that they were not key-words of Jesus' teaching ministry; that they are found relatively little in the Synoptic Gospels is of no significance. Such teaching is wholly compatible with the Synoptic record, and the editor of the Fourth Gospel I take to be nearer to an eye-witness than the other Gospels which, even if earlier in time, are further from the events which they narrate.

VIII. 21–59. This long controversial section we read, I think with some discomfort; it seems unreal, discordant, a mere wrangle, unlike the habit of the Jesus of the Synoptic records. We have a mental picture of Jesus on the hill-side, or from a boat, addressing crowds that listened attentively and respectfully to his words. The memories of John I are rather of days in Jerusalem of controversy, of tension, of bitter division of opinion. It is, no doubt, possible to hold that the whole passage is an invention of John II based upon controversies with the Jews in Ephesus or wherever this Gospel may have been written. But it does not, to my eyes, read in the least like the form local controversy is likely to have taken after the destruction of Jerusalem. Barrett writes: "John, it appears, is working with primitive Christian material, but," he adds, "he has deepened it and sharpened its edge".* I should rather say that he has translated his memory of John I's reminiscences into his typical Johannine phraseology. I have, therefore, once again presumed to retranslate or, rather, paraphrase the words of John II into a form that might well have come from John I, using, as always, the most colloquial language, partly because the passion and pleading of the voice of Jesus cannot be reproduced in words, and partly because John I so vividly remembered an actual historical occasion.

The Synoptists represent Jesus as foretelling his death and resurrection in the clearest terms, but it is obvious, as a matter of history, that when he died the disciples were not expecting a resurrection and were at first incredulous. It seems probable that during his lifetime he warned his close followers of his impending death and, in cryptic terms, told them that somehow he would

* op. cit. p. 276.

come back to them. Jesus' acceptance of his death as in some way necessary for the coming of the kingdom was an act of staggering faith. We should be wrong to assume that he knew how he was to come back; he knew only that God would vindicate his faith if he were faithful. His cryptic references to his coming back were interpreted by New Testament writers and the early Church in two different ways, which are never combined in the New Testament itself. Some took him to be referring to the Resurrection, others to the Parousia "on the clouds of heaven".* In the passage before us, perhaps because Jesus is arguing in public, not comforting his close followers, he speaks only of his going away.

It will be convenient to print the rest of my paraphrase directly in dialogue form. It would be reasonable to suppose that Jesus is addressing a generally sympathetic audience, but is interrupted by voices from the crowd which I here call 'the Pharisees'. We must try to imagine his voice and tone. I conceive that he spoke with terrible earnestness, yet always with pleading and compassion.

Jesus: I have only a little time left; I am going away, and where I am going you cannot follow me. You must make up your minds now; the decision whether you trust me or not is spiritually a matter of life and death to you (v. 21).

The Pharisees: What does he mean by that? Is he contemplating suicide? (v. 22).

Jesus: In the name of God I am offering you the light of life; to reject this offer is spiritual death (vv. 23 f.).

The Pharisees: Who are you to talk to us like this? (v. 25).

Jesus: I have never made any claims on my own behalf. I am simply telling you what I have been told by him that sent me, and I am certain of him who sent me (vv. 25 f.).

The Pharisees: Well, who is it that sent you? (v. 27).

Jesus: You will know the answer to your questions one day. I do nothing on my own; everything that I say to you I have learnt from the Father, and because I am obedient to him in all my mission, he never leaves me alone; he is always with me (vv. 28 f.).

Those whom I am here describing as 'the Pharisees' might

* *v.* Dodd, op. cit. p. 414.

better be called 'voices from the crowd', for many (we cannot guess what proportion of his hearers) were conscious that he was indeed speaking to them in the name and with the authority of God (v. 30). To these he says:

Jesus: Follow me; accept my word; then you will know the truth for yourselves, and the truth shall make you free (vv. 31 f.).

The Pharisees: But we are free already; the Romans may exercise political power, but the descendants of Abraham are God's freemen. What do you mean by saying that we shall be made free? (v. 33).

Jesus: No man is free who is in bondage to sin. As descendants of Abraham you may be serving in God's house, but you are only servants; you have not the freedom of the home as his true children have. I know that you are the children of Abraham with all that this involves of privilege, but you are not at home like children in your Father's house; if you were, you would not be plotting to get rid of me. I am telling what I have seen of the Father; listen to what I tell you, then, and follow his word as I do (vv. 34–38).

The Pharisees: You are always talking about 'the Father'; our father is Abraham (v. 39).

Jesus: If you were true children of Abraham, you would hear and obey the voice of God, as Abraham did; you would not be plotting against me. I have spoken the truth to you as God has revealed it to me. You are not open to the voice of the living God, as was Abraham (vv. 39–41).

The Pharisees: We are no bastard sons of Abraham; we are not Samaritans; we do not come from Galilee of the Gentiles. If you put it like that, we recognise only one Father, God himself (v. 41).

Jesus: If you were true sons of God, you would recognise and welcome me, for it is the heavenly Father who sent me; it is his word that I speak, not my own. You cannot listen to me because you are really children of the great Deceiver. It is only he who suggests murder. He represents lying and deception; it is I who am dealing with reality and truth. You have no charge to bring against me; you will not, you cannot, listen to me because your eyes are blinded to spiritual reality when it is presented to you. God is speaking through me today, and you cannot hear his voice because you are not spiritually his sons (vv. 42–47).

The Pharisees: How right we were! You're a heretic; you're mad (v. 48).

Jesus: I am not mad. I am not concerned about myself and my reputation; I leave that to God who judges truly, but I assure you that whoever listens to my word shall enter now into the life of the world to come; death will have no meaning for him (vv. 49–51).

The Pharisees: Now we are quite sure that you really are mad. Abraham died; all the prophets died, and you tell us that if we accept your words, we shall escape their fate. What do you make yourself out to be? (vv. 52 f.)

Jesus: I am making no claims for myself; I claim only to be speaking in the name of God. You call him your Father, but you do not know him; you cannot recognise what his Fatherhood means. I am sure of what I say of him and of the kingdom which is upon you; I cannot deny what I know; I am loyal to what I have seen and heard. You accept the tradition that Abraham in vision foresaw the day of God's coming kingdom and rejoiced in anticipation of it. I am telling you that what Abraham foresaw is now coming to pass (vv. 54–56).

The Pharisees: Are you actually telling us that Abraham foresaw you, a young man like you? (v. 57).*

Jesus: I solemnly assure you that this kingdom of God which God has sent me to declare to you, and bring to you, is from everlasting to everlasting in the purposes of God; it was there in the mind of God before ever Abraham was born (v. 58).

At this, some of the crowd began to throw stones at him, but Jesus managed to slip away out of the temple into hiding.

This is, of course, a most hazardous and uncertain reconstruction. It may be claimed for it only, first, that it closely follows the text; second, that it is a possible scene and dialogue; third, that, had it taken place, it would be re-written and edited in Johannine style as we find it in the Gospel, and fourth, that it seems really impossible why it should have been invented by John II were it not a record of John I's vivid reminiscences.

IX. 1–16. I find it most difficult to imagine that this vivid, detailed, circumstantial story of the healing of the blind man is the literary

---

* Following some early Mss., but see Barrett, *ad loc.*

invention of the editor. It must come to us from John I, who himself was present in Jerusalem. It presumably relates to the early days of Jesus' ministry. The editor has told the story with his own embellishments, which I think we may detect.

There must have been very many blind men in Jerusalem at this time, whom Jesus saw in the streets and temple courts. We should assume that, by some mysterious insight, some sudden moving of his spirit, Jesus turned his attention particularly to this one case. Jesus' healings were not indiscriminate.

We have, of course, no means of diagnosing the medical cause of this man's blindness. It would not be difficult to find instances of the curing of cases of what we call 'hysterical' blindness, where the cause of the trouble is in the mind or soul, not in any physical defect.* I am not aware of any known case of the mental healing of any man born blind, but I think the statement that this man was blind from birth is an insertion by the editor to heighten the miracle, for had the man been blind from birth it is not likely that the disciples would have asked whether his illness was due to his own sin.

In answer to the question whether the blindness was due to the man's own sin or to his parents' sin Jesus replies: "to neither, but that the works of God may be manifested in his case". Precisely this might be said of many sick persons healed by modern medicine. (vv. 1–3).

The following verses, 4 and 5, I find obscure. Jesus is reported to say, "you and I must do the works of God while it is day; the night is coming when no one can work. While I am in the world, I am its light". It is difficult to see what Jesus could have meant, if he said, "the night is coming when no one can work". To the editor these words would be a reference to Jesus' coming death and, perhaps probably, to the ceasing of miracles of healing in the later Church. Again, Jesus' open claim, "I am the light of the world", is in the editor's style and really incompatible with the Synoptists. Jesus may have said, in effect, "The works of God are to be manifested in this case; you and I have to do the works of God, for the promised day has come at last; the sunshine of God's mercy is revealed; in the case of this blind man I have been sent to declare and to manifest the light." That was to say in substance,

* v. E. R. Micklem, *Miracles And The New Psychology*, (pp. 101 ff.).

115

though not in word, "I am the light of the world". Jesus, we may affirm, must have said that, though he cannot be supposed to have said it in those words.

We are not at liberty to suppose that the anointing of the man's eyes and the command to go to bathe in the pool of Siloam were a kind of hoax, since Jesus might just as easily have cured the poor man with a wave of the hand (vv. 6 f.). This was a treatment of the ailment, though from the point of view of modern medical science it was valueless; Jesus was to be accused of *working* on the Sabbath day, for this happened to be a Sabbath.

When the treatment was completed, and the man was walking about enjoying sight, there was much discussion; some were asking, "surely that's the blind fellow we've seen so often?" Others said, "No, it can't be; it must be someone very like him". And the man said, "I am indeed the man you knew as blind." He then went on to explain what "the man called Jesus" had done and had prescribed. "Where is he?" they asked. The man answered, "I don't know" (vv. 8–12).

Jesus had worked on the Sabbath. The people, or some of them, seem to have said, "this is a police matter; the law has been broken; the police ought to be informed", for the religious authorities were, subject to the Romans, the civil authorities as well. The poor man is therefore brought up, as we should say, in court. There was division of opinion on the bench. Some said, "this looks, indeed, like the work of a man of God, but he cannot be that, since he has broken the Sabbath". Others said, "things like this can't be done by a sinner". So they turn to the defendant and ask him what he has to say about the man who gave him his sight. "He is a prophet", he answered. But the court wants more evidence; the man's parents are sent for: "is this man your son? Was he really blind and, if so, how has he come to see now?" The parents are very anxious not to be mixed up in any police court matter. "He is certainly our son," they say, "and he certainly was blind, but how he got back his sight – we know nothing about that; it has nothing to do with us; he's of age; let him speak for himself" (vv. 13–34).

The editor inserts a note to the effect that the parents were anxious to dissociate themselves from anything Jesus did because the Sanhedrin had decided to excommunicate from the synagogue anyone who acknowledged him as Messiah (v. 22). This is antedating events. The fact that the editor knew so little about the historical situation himself, yet so often gives us the correct setting of Jesus' sayings, is corroborative evidence that the witness of John I is the source of his narratives.

The court wants more satisfactory evidence, so the blind man is recalled. "You must give thanks to God for your recovery," they said to him, "but we know that this fellow who, as you think, healed you, is only a sinner, a transgressor of God's law." The blind man may have been a beggar, as we are told, but the editor may have represented him as a beggar because of some confusion with the healing of the blind beggar told in the Synoptists (Luke XVIII. 35). The man himself speaks with such courage, dignity and confidence before the court that he gives the impression of being a person of some standing in the community. He answers the court, "I cannot say anything about that; all I know is that I was blind, and I can see now" (v. 25). The court, which wants to have convincing evidence that Jesus had broken the law by working on the Sabbath, asks the man again: "tell us exactly what he did; how did he open your eyes?" "I've already given you a full account," the man replied, "why should I go over it all again? Can it be that you yourselves are thinking of becoming followers of his?" (vv. 26 f.). The Sanhedrin, not at all accustomed to being addressed like that, expressed its anger. "It is you who are his follower," they said; "we are followers of Moses, and we know that God spoke to Moses, but we do not know where this fellow comes from" (vv. 28 f.). It might seem that the blind man, no less than his judges, had lost his temper. "Things have come to a pretty pass," he said, "when there is amongst you one with this strange gift, and you don't even know where he comes from! He has performed an unparalleled miracle. I know as well as you do that God does not listen to those who break his Law. It is no good telling me that this man is only a sinner; if he were not a good man, and God were not with him, he could not have done anything for me" (vv. 30–33). "You are a scoundrel," they said to him, "how dare you presume to teach us?" and they chucked him out (v. 34).

Jesus hears of this and finds the man. There follows a conversation which, as it stands in the Gospel, is really not intelligible. Jesus, we read, goes up to the man and abruptly asks him, "do you believe in the Son of Man?". "How can I," answers the man, "when I do not know whom you mean?" "He who stands before you," said Jesus, "is the Son of Man" (vv. 35-37). This term, the Son of Man, which is almost unintelligible in Greek, is rarely found in the Fourth Gospel which is translating the faith of the first Hebrew Christians into the language the Graeco-Roman world could understand. Its appearance here may, therefore, appear as a mark of authenticity, a quotation from John I himself. But we are presented with two difficulties; first, this abrupt question presupposes that Jesus had been speaking about the Son of Man and, second, even if we suppose the conversation greatly reduced and assume that Jesus had spoken about the Son of Man, we do not know, in spite of all the learned books that have been written on the theme, what the phrase meant upon his lips. I can only suggest, with all hesitation, a conversation somewhat along these lines which might well have taken place. "Do you believe," asks Jesus, "in the Promised One who is to bring in the kingdom of God?" "Yes," says the blind man, "but who is he?" "It was for this that I was sent," replies Jesus. "Yes," answers the man, "I do believe." But here I write without any confidence. (vv. 35-38.)

We are to understand that a crowd surrounded Jesus, including some of the Pharisees. "This is my mission," says Jesus, in effect, "to bring sight to the blind and to reveal the blindness of those who think they see." "Are you suggesting that we Pharisees are really blind?" the Pharisees ask. "If you were really blind," Jesus answers, in effect, "you would not be blameworthy; it is because you claim to have spiritual insight, that you have no escape from sin" (vv. 39-41).

If we may take the two conversations, with the blind man and the Pharisees (vv. 35-41), as genuine reminiscences, we must treat them as epitomes of much longer talks.

X. 1-21. We come now to a passage of very great difficulty and, as I think, of great confusion. The last three verses (19-21) tell us that there was disagreement among Jesus' hearers; many said, "he is possessed and is mad; why listen to him?" Others said, "this is not the language of one possessed; you don't mean to say that a man who is possessed by an evil spirit can open the eyes of the blind!" If these verses are not misplaced, belonging really to the passage discussed above, the editor wants us to understand that these verses (1–18) are part of the discussion with the blind man and the crowd.

We should not have guessed from the Fourth Gospel that Jesus normally taught in parables. Here, however, we have a quite straightforward parable (vv. 2–6, I omit verse 1 for the moment.) We see the shepherd coming to the gate of the large fold that shelters several flocks. The janitor recognises him and opens the door for him. The shepherd calls his sheep; he knows them all by name; when they are collected, he goes ahead, and the sheep follow him; when he calls them, they recognise his voice and follow; if a stranger calls them, they take no notice. The picture is quite clear. It is, no doubt, possible that to this parable Jesus added something about the distinction between the shepherd and the robbers who climb over the walls of the fold sheep-stealing (v. 1), but this verse goes better with verse 8, and its present place is, I suggest, unnecessarily confusing, for in a parable Jesus indicated one point, not several.

We are told in verse 6 that the hearers did not understand his parable, and the editor seems to intend the following verses, 7–18, as an interpretation of it. We shall have to consider later whether this explanation is purely Johannine, or whether it is based upon actual words of Jesus. If we take the parable in verses 2 to 6 as it stands, it would seem relevant to the meaning and to the context of the preceding words to the Pharisees. Spiritual things are spiritually discerned. Those who know that they are blind and need a healer will respond to the words of Jesus; they will recognise his voice and will follow him; other discordant voices will never come home to them as true, as the voice of God. If verse 1, about thieves and robbers, belongs in the parable, it will be a reference to his opponents, but this is perhaps unlikely. This is a parable. Jesus does not say here, "I am the good shepherd", but the parable plainly refers to his work and mission; that he is the good shepherd is indeed its meaning. This parable indicates the manner in which Jesus was bound to speak about himself, indirectly but plainly for those with spiritual insight.

In the following verses (7–10) Jesus is not the shepherd but the door. The metaphor has two applications. First it is contrasted with the thieves and robbers who, as verse 1 had indicated, try to enter the fold of the kingdom by some other means than the door kept by the janitor. Second, the door is spoken of as open to the followers of Jesus, who are free to pass in and out and find pasturage, for Jesus has come to bestow life, abundant life. These verses are no explanation of the preceding parable. Are they wholly Johannine, or can we detect beneath them what Jesus may himself have said?

In the Synoptists Jesus is reported to have spoken of the straitness of the gate and the narrowness of the passage that leads to life eternal (Matt. VII. 13 f.; Luke XIII. 24). It is, therefore, intrinsically likely that he spoke of the door or gateway into the kingdom. Those who would enter must put away all their pretensions and thought of claims, and must enter with the humility of little children. The way to enter was to accept him as the appointed witness and messenger of God. In other words, though it is not to be thought that he himself put it in these terms, he was himself the door. For those who accept him, the door of their Father's house is ever open; they have the freedom of the sons of God.

If Jesus spoke of all those that were before him as thieves and robbers, he certainly could not have been referring to the great Hebrew prophets or the Baptist. There were plenty of pretenders such as Judas the Gaulonite or Barabbas to whom he might be referring; but the editor may be supposed to have had in mind the heresiarchs who were troubling the church in Asia in his time.

Verses 11–18 expound the text, "I am the good shepherd". Here, as throughout this Gospel, the evangelist reproduces not what Jesus actually said, but what he was really saying. It is entirely possible that Jesus, in his parabolic manner, may have contrasted the paid hand with the true shepherd who will not hesitate to risk his life for the sheep. He may, for instance, have used this illustration when he warned his followers that in going up to Jerusalem with him they risked their lives; here we can only surmise (vv. 11–13), but the following verses, 14–18, must certainly be regarded as Johannine. These things Jesus said only in the sense that he implied them. This is how the Church correctly understood him.

X. 22–42. In the Synoptists we often have great confidence that some genuine and reliable tradition of Jesus is before us, but – apart from the Passion narrative – we are hardly ever given any satisfactory indication of the when, the why, the how, the circumstances and the emotional tensions of any saying or of any deed. Here again, in X. 22–39, we have a scene, wholly in Johannine style, be it admitted, yet so circumstantial that either we have a reminiscence of John I written up by the editor, or the editor had the gifts and touch of a good novelist.

The occasion is the Feast of Dedication, which fell in November or December, and Jesus was walking in the shelter of Solomon's colonnade, as it was called, on the east side of the outer court of the Gentiles. 'The Jews', by whom the editor means the authorities, surround him and say to him, "how long are you going to keep us in suspense? If you are the Messiah, say so openly." Jesus refuses directly to answer the question, but speaks of his relationship with the Father and asserts "I and the Father are one" (v. 30). At that his opponents pick up stones to lynch him, on the ground that Moses demands death by stoning for blasphemy; but Jesus quotes to them from the 82nd psalm (v. 6), "I have said, Ye are gods; and all of you are children of the most High." What blasphemy is there, then, in his claim to be "a son of God" (v. 36)? There is a move to arrest him, but once again Jesus makes good his escape.

In the Johannine version of the story there are references back to the depicting of Jesus as the good shepherd (vv. 26–29), with emphasis on the claim that none can steal his sheep from the good shepherd. This reference to the shepherd does not fit the scene, and these verses give rather the assurance of the Church than any words Jesus can be supposed to have used on this occasion. These sentences, then, I omit as Johannine. Apart from them, does the incident ring true as historically possible or likely?

First, could Jesus who, it is to be thought, carefully avoided making public claims for himself, have declared, "I and the Father are one"? That could be said as well in Aramaic as in Greek (the word for 'one' would be *had* in Aramaic), but what would it mean if Jesus said it? If it be taken in a metaphysical sense as if Jesus were identifying himself with the Lord, the God of Israel, the charge of blasphemy would lie against him; but such a claim

121

upon the lips of a Jew is inconceivable. The words may, however, be taken in a religious, not a metaphysical sense. An Englishman might quite naturally say, "I and my friends are one in rejecting the doctrine of *apartheid*"; this would be an expression of spiritual or intellectual unity. In this sense Jesus might indeed have spoken of himself as one with the Father.

I will, therefore, once again re-write the Johannine story in my colloquial terms, suggesting what may well have been in John's reminiscence which the editor, in his own way, has retold.

The scene is the temple on a cold day in winter; Jesus is sheltering in one of the colonnades of the outer court. The authorities are determined to bring matters to a head; they surround him and say, in effect, "here you are going about teaching people and raising a great deal of excitement and perplexity; what is it all leading up to? Are you going to put forward claims to be the national Messiah? Come out into the open; tell us who you really think you are." To this Jesus replies that he has been concealing nothing; like the prophets before him he has been speaking to the nation in the name of the Father; if they will not recognise the authority of his words, at least his works of healing may be seen as God's corroboration of his message and his calling. He has spoken the words of the Father, he has done the deeds of the Father; he and the Father are one. When he said that, some of those present picked up stones to hurl at him, but Jesus reminds them that his work had been wholly beneficent, as everybody could see; what justification have they for picking up stones? "It is not for what you have done," they shouted, "it is for what you have said. You have identified yourself with God." Jesus reminds them of the text in the psalms which reads, "I have said, you are gods"; what blasphemy is it if he has claimed to be a son of the heavenly Father? If they could really say that the deeds he had done were not the works of God, let them reject him. Even if they refused to recognise his personal authority, they must recognise the works of God which proved that God was working through him, and that he was living in touch with God.

The charge of blasphemy plainly would not stand; "let us get him arrested", his enemies said, but before the police could arrive Jesus had managed to slip away. He escaped this time, but plainly a public ministry in Jerusalem was, for the time being at least, impossible for him. He retired into the lonely country beyond Jordan, where the Baptist had laboured. Here he was followed by a few. "The Baptist never did miracles like this", they said; "everything John said about Jesus was true," and they gave their allegiance to Jesus (X. 40–42).

It is most unlikely that my account of the scene is accurate, but something like this may well have occurred and been told by John. It is only by reading between the lines of the Synoptists that we get this sense of the peril of assassination in which Jesus stood.

XI. 1–57. The story of the resurrection of Lazarus has raised unbearable perplexities for the modern mind. The fact that this 'miracle', the supreme 'miracle', is not recorded in the Synoptists should not trouble us unduly. We have no reason to suppose that Peter and the Galilean disciples whose traditions we have in the Synoptists were present at the scene recorded in the last chapter, or were with Jesus in his retirement beyond Jordan. But brought up, as we are, in a scientific age we find it almost impossible to believe that a man who has been dead for four days can be brought back to life. The story is, therefore, generally regarded as a composition by the editor, who would lead up to the great climax, "I am the resurrection and the life". Howard, for instance, thinks we should regard the deep distress of Jesus (v. 33) as "the Johannine equivalent of the Synoptic record of the Agony in Gethsemane".* It is puzzling that the Greek word used here naturally or inevitably connotes indignation. Profound emotion is clearly portrayed. That Jesus raised the dead is asserted by the Synoptists in the case of Jairus's daughter (Mark V. 22–43) and the widow's son of Nain (Luke VII. 11–17), but in none of these cases is any medical evidence available to us, and the modern mind almost inevitably rejects the idea as impossible.

I am working on the assumption that the editor never, or hardly ever, quotes directly what John said; he reproduces John's reminiscences as he interprets them in the light of the thought-forms and faith of the later Church. Of this the story of Lazarus, culminating in the confession, "I am the resurrection and the

* Interpreter's Bible, ad loc.

life", is a supreme example; but, rejecting the view that the editor would have made a first-rate novelist, I am also assuming that a genuine reminiscence lies behind the story, and ask whether it is possible in any degree, or with any confidence, to divine what it may have been.

We may claim to see an editorial addition, almost certainly inaccurate, in verse two. We may be sure that Jesus did not, in so many words, declare that he is the resurrection and the life, and that Martha's confession of faith (v. 27) is in terms of later Church theology. I will venture, then, again in my colloquial terms, to retell the story as John may have told it to his friends in his old age.

"I very well remember that when Jesus had been teaching quietly the few beyond Jordan, he got a message from Mary and Martha that his friend Lazarus, their brother, was very ill. Jesus said, 'he is not dying; he will recover to the glory of God'. He was greatly attached to that family, and after a couple of days he said to us, 'let us return to Judaea'. We said to him, 'Master, the authorities nearly stoned you a short while ago; do you really propose to venture back into Judaea?' He then said something about it being always safe to work in the daytime. He saw that we were unpersuaded, so he said, 'our friend Lazarus has fallen asleep'. 'That's excellent news,' we said; 'if he has fallen asleep, he is sure to get better,' but we had misunderstood him, for he then said to us quite plainly, 'Lazarus has died, and I must go to the family.' Then Thomas spoke for us: 'we had better go with him, though we shan't come out of it alive'. Bethany, you know, is only a mile or two from Jerusalem. When we arrived we found that quite a crowd had come out from the city to show their sympathy with the sisters. When we got word to Martha that Jesus had come, she hurried to meet him. Mary stayed with the mourners. Martha said to Jesus, 'Master, if you had been here, this would never have happened.' Jesus said to her, 'but you know death is not the end'. 'Yes,' said Martha, 'I know that, but it is not much comfort to know that my brother will rise on the Last Day.' Jesus said to her, 'but you haven't understood what I have been teaching you; you have not realised and believed that the kingdom of God is really come upon you now; the old separation between this world and the world to come has been done away; you can't see Lazarus any more, but you haven't lost him. Don't you believe that?' 'Yes, Master,' she answered, 'I trust you; I do believe that.' Then she went back home and whispered to Mary, 'the Master is here; he wants to see you'. Mary at once slipped out to see him. Jesus who, of course, was anxious not to be observed, had not entered the village. But Mary could not get away unnoticed; people supposed she had gone to mourn at the tomb; she was therefore followed by the company who had gathered in sympathy. When Mary saw Jesus, she threw herself at his feet and said, 'Master, Lazarus would never have died if you had been here.' When Jesus saw the tears of Mary and the others he was terribly distressed and said, 'where have you put him?' They asked him to come and see. Jesus broke into tears himself. Seeing this, people said, 'how fond he was of him!' but there were those who said, 'he opened the eyes of the blind man; why couldn't he have prevented this death?' Jesus, then, was obviously greatly moved as we came to the burial place; it was a cave, and a big stone covered the entrance. To our astonishment Jesus said, 'roll the stone away'. Martha said, 'Master, we can't do that; you don't realise, he's been dead four days.' Jesus said to her, 'haven't I told you that if you have faith you shall see the glory of God? You people, move the stone away.' Jesus stood in front of the tomb, and we could see him praying; then he cried in a loud voice, 'Lazarus, come out!' And Lazarus came stumbling out with the shroud still wrapped round him and the handkerchief over his face. And Jesus said, 'get him out of those things and let him go home'."

I do not offer this as a correct account of John I's reminiscence, but I have told a possible story that might underlie John II's account of the occasion. But what of the miracle? Did Jesus really raise the dead? We might call psychology in aid here, except that psychology can help relatively little. Our psychologists have to speak about telepathic communication and clairvoyance, however inexplicable these things remain. I submit that there is no psychological, and therefore no scientific, difficulty in supposing that Jesus, hearing of Lazarus's illness, was convinced that he would recover, that later, perhaps by what we call clairvoyance, he saw the funeral procession of his friend and was convinced, therefore, that in spite of his presentiment of recovery Lazarus in fact had died. I suggest that the tears and terrible distress of Jesus were due to his conviction that Lazarus really was dead, and possibly to self-reproach that he had not come earlier, but that, when he got to the tomb, some faint sound or, more probably, some sixth sense made him certain that Lazarus was not dead but had been in a coma. Lazarus was presumably still unconscious but, hearing the beloved and imperious voice of Jesus, he rallies and stumbles out of the cave. I see some possible corroborative evidence that Lazarus was, in fact, alive, in that he could not have got out of the cave if he had not already kicked his legs free.

My reconstruction is hazardous, and most uncertain, but I put it to the reader that it is far more probable than that a novelist-editor invented the whole story. The sequel, verses 45 to 53, follows naturally, and is much too particularised to be an editorial invention. Jesus, one gathers, had hoped to see the two sisters privately, but he had not been able to escape the company of mourners; it was bound to be known at once in Jerusalem that he was back again. Some of those present were profoundly moved by what they had witnessed; others said, "we must let the authorities know that he is back". We may assume that Jesus returned across Jordan as secretly as he had come.

When the news reaches Jerusalem, the Sanhedrin is hastily summoned. It was generally felt that the situation was highly precarious; it had political implications; if this man were allowed to get a great following, the Roman Government would be bound to hear of it, for any rumour of a popular movement or rising among this inflammatory people would be likely to make the Government remove the special privileges of self-government which the Jews enjoyed. It was Caiaphas who put the general feeling. "We have no clear case against this man," he seems to have said, "that is, he has done nothing which would seem criminal in the eyes of Roman law, but he is a danger to our whole national position; we must get rid of him at all costs." This was the moment, therefore, when the Sanhedrin formally decided that Jesus must be killed.

From this story we once again derive a picture of Jesus such as we should hardly gather from the Synoptic writers. He was indeed the friend of all men, but, like us, he had his own special friends. To come to their help and comfort in their distress he literally risked his life. When he saw their sorrow, he was overwhelmed with distress, and then, as I think, it came to him that after all Lazarus was not really dead but in a coma. We may wonder whether Lazarus would, or could, have responded to any less commanding and imperious voice.

Jesus, we are told (v. 54), retired to a village called Ephraim on the borders of the desert country. It is surely to be thought that the editor would never have heard of the place if John I had not mentioned it, for from the point of view of the readers in Asia it was a totally meaningless and pointless detail. Jesus stayed there with his friends till Passover time. When the crowds began to gather in the city for the Passover, there was much talk about him. They looked for him in the temple and could not find him. "What do you think?" they said, "will he risk coming up to the Feast this year?" For it was well known that the authorities had asked to be told if he were seen; they intended to have him at once arrested (vv. 54–57).

XII. 1–11. Jesus has decided to go up to the feast, though it must involve his certain death. It says something for the courage and devotion of his close followers that they went up with him. He spends the night at Bethany. A little dinner-party, as we should call it, is arranged in celebration of Lazarus's marvellous return to life. Martha was in charge of the proceedings, but Lazarus was so far recovered as to be able to share in the meal. As part of the celebration Mary opened a bottle of extremely fragrant and expensive ointment and anointed Jesus. Judas of Kerioth with singular lack of manners and of spiritual sensitivity protests that this is a disgraceful waste of money, which had far better been spent in charity. "Don't interfere with her," says Jesus, "but let her keep the rest of it for my funeral." The Greek word for 'keep' is very puzzling here. I have added "the rest of it" to make sense. We should possibly take the sentence for a question, "do you want her to keep it for my burial?"

Up to a point the story is convincing. It is given in a different form by Mark (XIV. 1–9 cf. Matt. XXVI. 1–13). Commentators have pointed out a rather curious identity of phraseology between the two accounts in the description of the ointment, particularly the use of the adjective *pistikes*, the meaning of which we do not know; it may mean 'pure' or 'liquid' or it may be a corruption of the trade name of the ointment.* It is significant that Mark speaks of the ointment being poured upon the head, not the feet of Jesus. There is in Luke (VII. 36–50) another story of the prostitute who anointed the feet of Jesus and wiped them with the hairs of her head. In general, according to the hypothesis upon which I am working, the Fourth Gospel as being nearer to an eye-witness is to be preferred as an historical record to the Synoptists, but here I think John II's memory has failed him. He remembered John I's story of the anointing but mixed it up in his mind with the already traditional story of the woman in Luke who anointed the feet of Jesus and dried them with her hair; for in the first place, it is much more likely that at this celebration Mary anointed the head, not the feet of Jesus (Mark has this detail right, though his setting of the story is far less circumstantial than is this before us), and, in the second place, it is not really imaginable that a respectable woman at her own table at a celebration would under any circumstances unbind her hair.

There is, or there may be, a further reason why we should deem the editor to have misrepresented John I when he says that it was the feet of Jesus which Mary here anointed. It concerns the part of Judas of Kerioth. John II tells us that Judas was a thief and used to pilfer from the bag in which he carried such money as the party had. This we should probably take as his supposition rather than John I's reminiscence. It is not very likely that Judas would have been still entrusted with the bag, if he was known to purloin from it, and there was little time for the discovery to be made later. Judas became the traitor. We are told (XVIII. 2 f.) that he betrayed to the authorities where Jesus might be found after the Last Supper. This seems odd. It suggests a strange incompetence in the Jerusalem police. Either Jesus always went to the Mt of Olives to spend some time there after the evening meal, in which case the police, who were watching for him, would surely have discovered this for themselves, or Jesus did not habitually go there, in which case Judas could not have foreknown that he would be found there later. We are certainly given to understand that Judas made his arrangement with the authorities before the supper. The suggestion has been made that the information which Judas

* *v.* Preussen-Bauer, *Wörterbuch.*

really gave to the auth
evidence against Jesus, w
King in Bethany. This is hi
this anointing was not brou
called as witness, but it is po
possible that Jesus realised the da
recognised what Judas saw in it,
anointed him not for kingship bu

Be that as it may, Jesus' arrival
secret in the village. A number of pe
both to see Jesus and to see Lazarus
news quickly got to Jerusalem, and th
they had better get rid of Lazarus wel

Mark did not know, what John remem   at this
meal was a family celebration. When Mary   the bottle of
very expensive ointment, and Judas said,   .vnat a waste of
money!", Jesus said, in effect, "No, you mustn't say that. It is
always a duty to give to the poor, but deeds are more eloquent
than words; I know what Mary means, and I accept it."

XII. 12–19. Next day the rumour quickly spreads that Jesus is
going up to the feast. The editor says (v. 18) that a crowd came
out to meet him from Jerusalem; it is much more probable that,
as the Synoptists have it, and as would be consistent with v. 12,
he was accompanied by those who were staying in Bethany.
Everyone had heard of the raising of Lazarus; the excitement was
very great. The people cut branches from the palm-trees and
accompany Jesus, calling out, "Save now! Blessed is he that comes
in the name of the Lord!" It was in the name of the Lord that
Jesus had come like the prophets before him. The additional
words, "even the king of Israel", which are no part of the Biblical
quotation, we may safely regard as an editorial addition pointing
forward to the following quotation from Zechariah (v. 15). As
Dr Barrett comments, if the disciples did not understand the
Messianic significance of the entry, *a fortiori* neither did the crowd.

We are not told in this Gospel of the careful preparation Jesus
had made that a donkey should be available for him (Mark
XIV. 12 ff.). This story in the Synoptists presupposes friends and

salem such as we learn of in this Gospel
At the time his friends had no sense of the
his entry into Jerusalem riding upon a donkey; it
that they recognised the fulfilment of the Messianic
cy. Jesus enters the city amid a crowd of people excited
chiefly by the raising of Lazarus. The authorities are very much
alarmed by this popular demonstration, but they had as yet no
grounds for any action.

The "Triumphal Entry", as we call it, we are apt to miscon-
ceive. Had Jesus really entered the city amid a crowd shouting
"here comes the king of Israel", the temple police would have
been bound at once to intervene, and later the authorities would
have no difficulty in producing political evidence which they
could bring before the Roman Governor. But we have good
reason to be sure that his entry riding upon a donkey, though at
the time it had no significance for his followers, had great significance for Jesus himself, since he had made careful provision for it.
It may be that we have here an almost unique glimpse into his
mind. A little earlier, when he was in danger of being lynched, he
had withdrawn into hiding or retirement beyond Jordan, "for his
hour had not come yet". But with this new Passover feast his
time was come. He was under no illusion that he could escape his
enemies. It is possible that he expected to meet his death by stoning, and that the ultimate horror of the Romans being brought
into it and of the crucifixion was hidden from him still, but we
cannot know. He is to make his last appeal to his people; he is to
die for them. There is to be for them no Messiah such as they hoped
for and expected. He has meditated long and often on the text,
"behold, thy king cometh unto thee meek and riding upon an
ass"; this is the only king, the only Messiah, they are to know; it
is he himself who must fulfil the prophecy. We can perhaps dimly
imagine, then, his feelings as he mounted the donkey and started
on his journey. The Synoptists tell us (Luke XIX. 41) that when
he caught sight of the city, he completely broke down: "If only
you had known, on this great day, the way that leads to peace!
But no; it is hidden from your sight."* He went on to predict
the utter destruction of Jerusalem till not one stone was left
standing upon another, "because you did not recognise God's

* *New English Bible.*

moment when it came." He loved his people with an unutterable love, and must die for them, and nobody understood it in the least.

He may have been glad that he was accompanied by an enthusiastic if uncomprehending crowd, for, almost certainly, the first thing he did was to go into the temple, drive out the cattle and money-changers and claim the temple as a house of prayer for all nations. This he did by the majestic force of his own personality, but he could hardly have done it in the presence of an angry and hostile crowd. This story has been given out of place and earlier in this Gospel.

XII. 20–30. The story of the Greeks who wished to see Jesus (vv. 20–24) passes without a break into the general account of these last days. Many Greek-speaking Jews of the Diaspora came up to the festival. Some of these approach Philip, who, though he came from Bethsaida, had a Greek name and presumably could understand Greek. They ask for an interview with Jesus. Philip consults Andrew, and they approach Jesus together. Why should Philip have to consult Andrew? We have no reason to suppose that Jesus refused to talk with any who approached him now; we may perhaps reasonably guess that these Greek-speaking Jews wanted to invite Jesus to visit them abroad. It would be quite natural in this case that Philip should think he had better consult Andrew first. Moreover, this supposition gives point to Jesus' answer. He cannot contemplate a journey abroad, however urgent, for, as he says in his parable, a grain of wheat must fall into the ground and *die*, if it is to be fruitful.

This may, or may not, have been the occasion when Jesus, as reported elsewhere also (Matt. X. 39. Luke XIV. 26, XVII. 33), spoke of the man who holds on to life at all costs as the man who loses it, whereas he who risks his life now finds eternal life (v. 25), and he may have added, in effect, "if any man would be a follower of mine, let him stand by me now, and he will receive honour from God" (v. 26).

We are, I think, to understand that this appeal from the Greek-speaking Jews was an almost overwhelming temptation to Jesus. It would be, as we might put it, a perfectly honourable escape from an impossible and desperate situation. The Greek-speaking Jews of the Diaspora in Egypt and elsewhere tended to be far more liberal in their outlook than the ecclesiastical authorities in Judaea. In Alexandria, in Athens or in Babylon he might hope for a far more sympathetic and understanding hearing; would it not be better, even at this last moment, to abandon his hopeless project in Jerusalem and take his message to a more sympathetic audience? Jesus, we might say, reeled under the temptation; his prayer was an agony of spirit. We cannot know whether he prayed out loud, but we cannot doubt that we are given the very substance of his prayer: "Father, save me from this hour; yet it was for this hour that I came. Father, thy name be glorified." It may well be that at this moment there was a thunder-clap. The people, vaguely aware of his agony of mind, said "an angel is speaking to him". Jesus said to them, in effect, "No, this is not an angel speaking to me, but it is a sign to you that God has heard my prayer."

XII. 31–50. The following verses, 31–36, as they stand are plainly Johannine. It is a question whether beneath them we can guess what Jesus may well have said. That he spoke of the casting out of Satan seems certain (v. 31); he spoke of his only being with them a little time more (v. 35 cf.), and declared that his message, received or repudiated, was a judgement upon his hearers (v. 31). But he can hardly have said that he "if he be lifted up" would draw all men to him with a reference to the crucifixion, for even if he himself anticipated crucifixion, his words would have been a riddle to his hearers, unless possibly, as has been suggested to me, there were an underlying reference back to Gen. XL. 13, 19. The editor in a sense corrects himself (v. 34), for the crowd asks what he means by the lifting up of "the Son of Man". In the famous passage of Daniel (VII. 13 f.) the "one like a man" is the representative of the kingdom of the saints which is to succeed the rule of the pagan kingdoms represented by wild beasts. The Man or Son of Man is raised up to receive the kingdom from the hands of God, and it is at least quite possible that Jesus in this sense used the term "Son of Man" and could speak of the Son of Man being lifted up. If he said that he had only a little time left, people may well have said, "then he cannot be the promised Messiah, because we know that Messiah's reign will have no end" (v. 34). Jesus, as we have seen before,* may well have spoken of his message as the great light shining upon them that sat in darkness and exhorted his hearers to walk in the light and no longer stumble about like blind men; let them trust in the light and become sons of light (vv. 35 f). But whether Jesus actually said such things at this time is a matter of speculation.

We certainly shall not doubt, however, that when the work of this day was done Jesus went into hiding either in a friend's house or outside the city (v. 36). We should gather from the following verses, 37–43, that he had met with relatively little response; this is the point of the editor's reference to the passages which he quotes from the prophet Isaiah. On the other hand, some, even among the authorities, believed that he spoke a word from God, but they kept quiet lest they be involved in the fate they feared for him.

In the next verses, 44–50, we have in Johannine, and therefore technically in unhistorical, dress what Jesus was always saying. We have a picture of him which we may take as surely historical, though we derive it from the Synoptists only by implication. I will paraphrase it in colloquial terms and a form that is credible and even necessary historically. "I am not making any personal claims; it is in God that I call you to put your trust; if you have seen that which I have been declaring to you, you have seen what God is revealing to you of himself. It is the light shining upon those that sat in darkness which I bring you; trust me, and you will no more walk in darkness. It is not for me to judge those who reject my words; they are judging themselves as they will know one day. It is for your salvation that I have been sent. I am not offering you my private opinions; it is God himself who sent me and put his words in my mouth; he has laid his hand upon me and told me what I must say, and I know from experience that to accept this word of his is to enter into true life. I am only the mouthpiece of God."

If this bare paraphrase in any way truly represents what Jesus said, it is important from two aspects. First, Jesus made no claims for himself except that he had been sent. Here he stands directly

* *v.* p. VIII, 12 *supra.*

133

in the line of the Hebrew prophets and in contradiction of the whole setting of John II's Gospel. Second, we rarely get from the Synoptists this sense of pressure, of urgency, of personal force as of one who speaks with terrific conviction under stress of an overwhelming sense that his utterance is a word to men from God himself. In the Synoptists are recorded many sentences that Jesus uttered; in this kind of way the Fourth Gospel is quite unreliable, but, on the other hand, through its form and linguistic usages we can, as it were, *hear* the passion and the power with which he spoke.

XIII. 1–30. There has been much discussion as to why John II in his account of the Last Supper makes no direct reference to the breaking of the bread and the sharing of the cup together with the words then spoken by Jesus. The answer to this question, as suggested by the hypothesis I am following, may be quite simple. John II, I am assuming throughout, is basing himself upon John I's reminiscences, but these he has taken and translated into a language more familiar to the Graeco-Roman world and better accommodated to the developing theology of the Church in Asia. This he could not do with the eucharistic words and acts of Jesus; these, repeated by the Church Sunday by Sunday, were, at least relatively, fixed and were not open to retranslation. It may be said that in speaking of Jesus as the Bread of Life (Ch. VI) and, later, as the true Vine (XV. 1ff) the editor has in his own way translated the words of Jesus here, but the event itself, which had become the familiar church rite he could not directly handle in his usual way. This might be the explanation.

It seems to be a view widely held among scholars that the *pedilavium* or foot-washing never actually took place, that it was invented or constructed by John II upon the basis of such Dominical sayings as, "but I am among you as he that serveth" (Luke XXII. 27), and, further, that he has meant it as a commentary on the rite of baptism. Such hypotheses cannot be disproved. One may raise the question whether John II would have dared to invent this story if it were not based on Church tradition. It is, I venture to suggest, more difficult to understand why the Synoptists omitted this story than why the Fourth Gospel makes no direct reference to the breaking of the bread. Here, at any rate, I shall treat the story as based on the reminiscences of John I.

Jesus knows that he has been sent by God; he has rejected the terrible temptation to accept the invitation of the Greek-speaking Jews; he has loved his own people in Jerusalem and Palestine; he will show his love for them to the very utmost; he will not leave them, though it will certainly cost him his life. (v. 1). Here as elsewhere I am translating the moving, devotional, hieratic language of John II into very colloquial English that the historical scene may the more clearly be visualised.

There are two important grammatical variants in verse 2. It was before a meal that a slave would remove the sandals of the guests and wash their feet. We should, therefore, confidently read with some manuscripts, "when the time for the meal had come", not "when the meal was now over". Second, we should very possibly translate, "when the devil had whispered to Jesus that Judas would betray him".

On this occasion there was no slave present to wash the feet of the guests. None of the disciples would volunteer; their concern was rather with precedence, who should be greatest in the kingdom of heaven. How little they understood him as yet! He had spoken to them about humility and service; they had said "Yes", but they had not really understood, and now he must leave them. An action will speak more loudly than any words. We might have thought that at a moment like this his mind would have been full of the imminent horror of what was coming to himself, but, as John II has put it (vv. 1 and 3), all that was behind him; it is of his disciples only that he is thinking. He proceeds to put on an apron and to perform the function of the slave. Peter violently protests, "*you* can't do that to *me*"; Jesus replies that he cannot see the significance of this now, but one day he will understand. "No," says Peter, "I will never let *you* wash *my* feet." Jesus says to him, "if you do not let me do this, you have no partnership with me". "Very well, in that case," says Peter, "wash my hands and my head too that I may wholly be your partner." "There is no need at all for that," says Jesus.

One may suspect that the reference to Judas here (v. 11) is anticipatory of vv. 21 ff. The editor would make it plain that the mere physical washing did not of itself make any man a partner

135

with Jesus: no man could be his partner who had not accepted him in the sense of receiving his spirit, the opposite of theirs who still quarrelled as to who should be greatest in the kingdom. They would never understand this unless he showed it to them in deed and not in teaching only. Verses 13–15 need no commentary and may indeed, for once, represent the very words of Jesus.

Verses 16–20 may be taken as Johannine comment, though put into the lips of Jesus and not in substance at variance with what he said at different times.

Jesus has washed their feet; he has told them that this is the kind of service they must do for one another; there is a new and wonderful feeling of intimacy. Then Jesus, in dreadful distress (v. 21), says to them, "but one of you is going to betray me". The disciples are utterly bewildered. "Whom does he mean?", they asked as they looked at one another. Peter makes a sign to John, "the disciple whom Jesus loved", who was next to Jesus at the table. "Ask him whom he means". At the Passover the participants lay on couches each resting on his left arm. John therefore being on his right would speak to him most easily and might be said to be lying "in his bosom". The place of honour was on Jesus' right. "By throwing back his head the disciple would be able actually to touch the chest of Jesus, and then to speak very quietly".* If this meal was not the Passover itself, as the Gospel states, we may assume that the table had been already laid in preparation for the Passover. John therefore leant over and whispered to Jesus, "who is it?" The sequel makes it quite plain that Jesus did not directly point to Judas. It may be he said, "It's one of you who are sharing this meal with me". It is not given us to imagine the strain under which Jesus stood. Some time later he whispers to Judas, "What you are going to do, do quickly" (v. 27). The disciples, who had no suspicion of Judas, thought that Jesus had sent him on some little shopping errand, and Judas slipped out, and it was night. It was night indeed!

XIII. 31–XIV. 31. Contains a long Johannine discourse which is not to be taken as an historical transcript of what Jesus said. The Synoptists give us only the briefest glimpse of what Jesus said and

* Barrett op. cit. p. 373.

did at that Last Supper; we have to supply the atmosphere from our own imagination. When Judas had gone off, Jesus knew that he had only a matter of minutes now with his friends. John I could never forget that night; he must often have talked of what Jesus said when Judas had left the party. To the theologian-editor the Passion of Jesus is the glory of Jesus; it is in such theological terms that he reproduces John's reminiscences as he remembers them. Our question is, how far we are able through the Johannine construction to divine what according to John's memory Jesus said, or must have said, in these few last minutes with his friends.

If we eliminate Johannine theology, we get an impression of what actually was said; I paraphrase; I use colloquial language; I am not presuming to say what Jesus said, but from this Gospel I get the clear impression that Jesus must have said something like this: "Brothers, we've only a few minutes left, then you will see me no more, for, as I said in the temple, I am going where you cannot come. Look, I am giving you a new commandment: you are to give yourselves to one another as I have given myself to you." Jesus in this commandment had summed up so much of what he so desperately wanted them to understand, but instead of taking this up Peter asks, "What is all this about your going away?" Jesus says to him, "where I am going, you cannot follow now, but you will follow one day". "Why can't I follow you now?", Peter protests; "I'd follow you to death." "I know you mean that," said Jesus, "but I warn you that before tomorrow morning you will repeatedly have denied that you have anything to do with me" (v. 38). How well Jesus knew his friends, and how little they knew themselves! He realised what an appalling shock to them would be his death which even now they did not anticipate. "Whatever happens to me, don't be troubled; you trust in God; well, trust in me too, that I know what I am doing, and that it is my Father's will. As in the temple there are the outer courts and the inner and then the sanctuary, so it is in the spiritual life. It is for your sakes that I must go away; I would have told you had it been otherwise, and I am coming back; we are not going to be permanently separated. You know the road you have to walk." But the disciples still cannot understand what he means by this mysterious saying, "I am going away from you", and Thomas protests, "but, Master, we don't know where you are going; we are your followers, how can we possibly know the road we should walk if we don't know where you are?" Jesus answered that question by saying in effect, but not in Johannine terms, that he was himself the Way, the Truth, the Life. As the writer to the Hebrews put it, Jesus has opened for us a new and living way into the sanctuary (X. 20). How Jesus put this to them now we cannot tell; he may have said, "in what I have taught you, and in what I have done in the name of the heavenly Father I have shown you the road to walk, I have revealed to you the real, the heavenly world about us and beyond, I have shown you the way of life; it is by accepting me and my words that you come to the Father". What was that but to say in other words, "I am the Way, the Reality, the Life"?

But what does coming to the Father mean? Perhaps it was this question that troubled Philip, and it was as if he said, "if only we knew what that meant, if only that came home to us, we should be satisfied" (v. 8). To this perhaps Jesus replied, "after all this time with me, Philip, have you not understood me yet? To have received my teaching, to have recognised my works as the works of God, to have identified yourselves with me and my cause, this *is* to know the Father." Such a reconstruction, which may cover vv. 9–11 is here offered with every hesitation. I do not accept the view that this whole passage is a literary device and invention of John II, but I agree that it is Johannine and therefore is not to be taken as accurate reporting. It would be reasonable to think that something like my reconstruction both rests upon the text and is appropriate to the occasion, and might therefore be near to the event itself.

Verses 12–14 may well rest upon what Jesus said in some form, but they seem here a little out of place, for vv. 15 ff. revert to the disciples' anxiety at Jesus' words that he was leaving them and going whither they could not follow. He may so well have said, "When I am gone, be loyal to all that I have told you (v. 15), and don't be afraid, for I am coming back, and God will not leave you like orphans without me, he will send you his Spirit to keep you straight and to comfort you; his Spirit will be within you; you will not be lost as the world is. I shall very soon be beyond the sight of man, but I shall not be lost to you; there is nothing that can separate us; be loyal, and the love of God will rest upon you, and you will realise that I am with you."

Judas, not the Judas from Kerioth, interrupted him at this point. "What do you mean, Master, by saying that you are passing beyond the sight of man, but that you will make yourself known to us?" (v. 22). To this Jesus may have replied in such terms as these (but with a passion and vividness very different from the banal language which I here ascribe to him): "be loyal to me when I am gone, and God will be with you, and I shall be with you – permanently. There is little I can say now; when I am gone, the divine Spirit will make all clear to you" (vv. 23–26).

I must pause to comment here. The editor is re-writing John's reminiscences, as I suppose, in the light of the later experience of the Church. The Synoptists much mislead us by saying that Jesus clearly foresaw his crucificion and resurrection. The Fourth Gospel is to be deemed much more historical. Here Jesus uses clear language about his going away and very vague language about what would happen then. Even at this point, it is plain, his friends did not anticipate his death, but it was his utter conviction that in the mysterious purposes of God he must go down to death for his people. What exactly would happen then, he did not know. Even his close friends still understood so little, as the need for the foot-washing had shown. It was by an utterly staggering act of faith in God, his Father, that he went to his death, "the author and finisher of faith", as one writer puts it (Heb. XII. 2). He tells his followers plainly that he is passing from the sight of man, but he comforts them by assuring them in vague terms (for the future he does not foresee) that if they are loyal to him, God will certainly not abandon them, and that in some way he will himself come back to them.

Verses 27–31. Judas has gone out to betray him; Jesus knows that he only has a short time on earth and only a few minutes with his friends; he is next door to death in some horrible form by violence, and the future he cannot foresee, for the purposes of God are hidden; he knows only that he must be obedient to the voice within – and he is at peace: "peace I leave with you, my own peace I give to you; this is the real peace, not the world's easy gift as it cries 'shalôm'.* Whatever happens, you are not to be afraid. I

* 'Peace' is also the word used for 'farewell'.

have spoken of my going away; if you realised, as I do, that my going is required by the Father for the salvation of men, you would have been glad, when I said I was going away. There is no time to say more now. I fulfil the will of my heavenly Father, and the forces of evil have no power over me. Come, we must be going now."

However inaccurate I be in detail, and however my words fall short of his, do we not here have a picture of the historical Jesus more intimate, more credible, than the figure in the other Gospels? It is as if these give us a magnificent statue of the Man of Nazareth, but the Fourth Gospel here pre-eminently gives us a living portrait.

XV. Unless chapters XV, XVI and XVII are misplaced by some accident to the original manuscript, they strongly confirm my view that John II was not a novelist. Jesus in Ch. XIV has spoken his last words to his friends and has said, "now we must be going". The story is continued in Ch. XVIII. In between, most unsatisfactorily from the dramatic or novelist point of view, we have three chapters of Johannine meditation. These cannot from our present point of view be neglected, for if the editor hardly ever gives us Jesus' words, he represents in his own idiom the significance of what he said.

Chapter XV is a meditation gathering round the theme of Jesus as the true vine. It repeats some earlier themes such as the command to the friends to love one another and the warning that his coming was for judgement in that, the light being now revealed, the rejection of the light was sin where no sin had been before.* The brief saying, "the slave is not greater than his lord", is probably a direct quotation of a saying of Jesus (v. 20).† He may well have called the disciples his friends (v. 14), but it is extremely unlikely that he had ever called them slaves (v. 15).

The main theme of the chapter, however, is the indwelling of the believer in Christ and Christ's indwelling in him. This rests upon the allegory that God is the gardener, Jesus the vine, and the disciples are branches. We have here the teaching and experience

* cf. *supra*. IX. 40f.
† cf. Matt. X. 24.

of the early Church. The vine or vineyard represents Israel in the Old Testament (Ps. LXXX. 8, Is. V. 1 cf. Matt. XXI. 33). This sentence may be paraphrased, "I am the true Israel". I think we may take it as certain that Jesus never directly said, "I am the genuine vine" (v. 1), partly because this was not his manner of speaking, and partly because the adjective used is somewhat philosophical, turning into an allegory what at first may well have been a parable. Plato spoke of the true or ultimately real world of which the things of sense are but a symbol or imperfect realisation. The text before us would mean that Jesus is himself the reality of which the vines that grow on earth are but the symbols. This would be a philosophical conception far removed from his Semitic thought.

But we should not conclude from this that the chapter is all of the editor's invention. In chapter XIV Jesus has spoken in some vague way of his going away and his coming back; even after he has gone, he will still be with his friends. This vague and authentic language has been misrepresented by the Synoptists, who sometimes say that he clearly announced his 'resurrection' on the third day, and sometimes, but never at the same time, speak of his Parousia on the clouds of heaven in terms of current Jewish apocalyptic. Jesus spoke in picture language, and I should not wish to claim that his alleged teaching about Resurrection and Parousia has no relation to anything he ever said, but we need not doubt that the general picture in the Fourth Gospel is more historical. Jesus spoke of his going away and of his somehow coming back, and greatly were his friends perplexed. The Fourth Gospel interprets his coming back in terms of the mutual indwelling of Jesus and his disciples. This is often taken as an indication of the Church's difficulty when his immediate and speedily expected return remained unrealised, but it may well be that the editor is simply representing in his own manner and idiom, not merely the actual experience of the Church, but an element also in the Master's teaching.

Jesus taught by parable, not allegory, but his parables soon came to be allegorically interpreted. From this allegory it is not difficult to infer a parable which would be in the style of Jesus' teaching. He may well have said something like this: "consider the vine-tree and the way the gardener tends and dresses, prunes and cleans it. The life of the branches depends wholly upon the life of the tree. A

141

branch is pruned that it may bear more fruit; a branch that is cut off from the tree withers away and is fit for nothing but for burning." That is the sort of parable from nature which Jesus often used.

If we may assume that Jesus uttered some such parable as I have suggested, what would he have meant by it? We can only guess at the context, but he might well have spoken such a parable as, for instance, when the people protested, "but we are all true sons of Abraham".* They are, indeed, all by descent sons of Abraham, Jesus would have replied, but only in so far as they abide in the faith of Abraham. This, indeed, is precisely what according to this Gospel he did say in other words. This might be put in the form, "you are true sons of Abraham provided that Abraham abides in you, and you abide in him". In this case the editor is stretching the words, but not in any way the meaning, of the parable when he speaks here of the abiding of Jesus in his friends and their abiding in him. The editor applies this parable, if there ever was such, to elucidate Jesus' meaning when he spoke so darkly of his somehow coming back. Nor is it at all impossible that Jesus spoke in some such terms when at the Last Supper he sought to answer the anxious question of his disciples. In all this anxious and repeated questioning about his coming back and Jesus' somewhat vague answers, we are, as I suppose, very near to history. The stupendous faith of Jesus in going to his death stands out the more clearly if we assume on the basis of this Gospel that he did not know precisely what would happen after his death. He could only trust in God.

XVI. This chapter is a further meditation. It is Johannine throughout. This does not mean that it is not true, for it plainly arises from profound Christian experience. We are concerned at the moment, however, solely with the question whether it is in any degree historical. The editor knew from experience that the Paraclete,† the Comforter, the Spirit had come; Jesus spoke now in the Spirit. To us of the modern world it seems important to know whether Jesus during his lifetime actually used the words ascribed to him,

---

* *supra.* VIII. 33.

† C. K. Williams translates "the Paraclete" as "the Friend" with a note that the word means "the prisoner's friend who speaks for him in court".

but to the editor that which Jesus said then and that which he says now are not to be distinguished; all are equally his words. Much Jesus could not say then but he was saying it now (v. 12); he spoke then in parables or hints; after his death and resurrection he spoke plainly (v. 29). The editor even makes Jesus say, "none of you asks me whither I am going" (v. 5), whereas it seems plain even from this chapter (v. 17) that this is precisely the question that troubled the disciples. The later Church knew well the answer.

Jesus, as we gather from the Synoptists, had warned his disciples that, if they came up with him to Jerusalem, they took their lives in their hands. Knowing that his death was imminent it is entirely possible that at the Last Supper he warned them that as his known followers their position would be hazardous, but the more particular warnings, as that they would be excommunicated from the synagogue or that anyone killing them would think he did God service (v. 2), must be taken as arising from the later experience of his followers. In this connection the words, "I did not tell you this at first because I was with you" (v. 4) may be revealing; it is true that the text continues, "but now I am going to the Father", but such an addition is almost necessary since the editor is purporting to tell what Jesus said on his last night with the disciples on earth. Jesus had much to say, but it would be beyond the grasp of his hearers at present; when he was gone, the Spirit would lead them into all truth (vv. 12 f.). The editor in composing his Gospel did not make that clear historical distinction between the utterances of Jesus then and now which modern historical thinking requires of us.

It seems to us with our hindsight incredible that the disciples should not have realised that Jesus was going to his death, but all of them, perhaps, with the exception of John, the disciple "whom Jesus loved" and who may possibly have been host at the Last Supper and as such took a place next to Jesus, came from Galilee. They may have been very ignorant of the state of feeling in Jerusalem. We revert again to his mysterious and enigmatic saying that he was going away. In his cryptic manner Jesus is reported to have said, "after a short time, you will not see me, and again after a short time you will see me" (v. 16). The disciples, we gather, whispered among themselves, "what does he mean?" (vv. 17). But at last, as we are given to understand, they receive an answer

143

that satisfies them. They are not told, however, about the resurrection on the third day or the Coming Again on the clouds of heaven. Jesus had told them only that he was sent from God and was returning to God (v. 28). "That makes everything clear", the disciples are made to say; "herein our faith rests sure that God sent you" (vv. 29 f.). It is as if Jesus had said to them, "I am going to death because I am convinced that this is the will of God. I trust him, and you must trust him too." It may have been on such an occasion that Jesus warned them, saying in effect, "you think you trust and that your faith is sure, but I know that when the crisis comes, you will all scatter, and I shall be left alone. There is terrible anguish ahead for you like that of a woman in travail, but you like her shall come to great joy when that is over" (vv. 32 f.).

XVII. The editor has taken upon himself to put into the lips of Jesus his prayer as he went to his final suffering. We must regard this chapter as a Johannine composition, for not only was there none to memorise or record this extended prayer, but it is impossible that in prayer to God, his Father, Jesus should have referred to himself as 'Jesus Christ' (v. 3) or said (v. 13) that his words were spoken in the world for the benefit of the hearers on earth. The recognition that this is a Johannine composition, however, does not render it of no devotional or spiritual significance or as untrue to the mind of Jesus. It is to be taken presumably as the Johannine rendering of the prayer in the Garden of Gethsemane recorded in the Synoptic Gospels.

The prayer requires few notes. Jesus, we observe, addresses God as 'Father' simply (vv. 1, 24) or as 'holy Father' (v. 11). This we may assume to be a correct tradition. Second, the word translated 'glory' or 'glorify' occurs in this chapter some seven times (vv. 1, 4, 5, 10, 22, 24). The 'shame' and 'scandal' of the crucifixion have become 'the glory'. Third, the word we translate 'truth' occurs in this chapter three times (vv. 17, 19). These two concepts, glory and truth or reality are key-words of Johannine theology, but it is not, so far as we know, in such terms that Jesus was wont to speak of his mission or himself. The very brief treatment of this moving chapter here is for the reason that it throws little light upon the purely historical question which is the subject of this book. "And this is life eternal, that they should know thee, the only true God, and Jesus Christ whom thou has sent" (v. 3), or, as it might be paraphrased, "to know the reality of God through Jesus Christ is to have entered into that life to which time is irrelevant". This is the summation of the Christian Gospel.

XVIII. 1–27. We come now to the Passion narrative which is found in all the Gospels but in divergent forms. The story as given in the fourth Gospel represents a very different tradition from that on which the Synoptists draw. It is the proper task of scholars and historians to compare and estimate the various accounts that come down to us and decide as best they can what was the true sequence of events. Into this necessary inquiry it is not my task to enter here. I am concerned solely with the reminiscences of John I as we may presume to infer them from the record of John II. I am remembering that John II's memory may possibly have been at fault, and that he was not dependent solely upon John I. I am not assuming that where the Synoptics differ from the Fourth Gospel, the latter must always be preferred, but it is important that John II gives us a straightforward and intelligible narrative, and that he probably had behind him the reminiscences of one who was actually present.

In respect of the arrest of Jesus, for instance (vv. 1–11), the editor is taken to assert that Roman troops were sent with the emissaries of the Sanhedrin to arrest Jesus. This view rests upon the fact that the Greek word *speira* is the Greek translation of the Roman 'cohort'; a cohort of some 600 men is said to have been sent under their tribune. This is not believable. On the other hand, Gardner-Smith writes: "Pilate may have been anxious not to intervene more than was necessary, as indeed appears from the record of the subsequent trial. His business was to keep order, no easy task at the Passover; and by sending a detachment of soldiers to reinforce the temple police he may have displayed no more than ordinary caution."* The matter is not important.

The party arrives. Judas, we are told, is with them. The Sanhedrin was anxious to avoid any possible public demonstration; Judas had told them where Jesus would probably be found (v. 2). Jesus goes out to meet them and asks, "for whom are you

* op. cit. p. 58.

looking?"; "for Jesus of Nazareth", they say. "I am he", replies Jesus. The editor then tells us that the company stepped back and tumbled on the ground. This is so unlikely that we must ascribe the tumbling to John II's imagination, but we could easily believe that when they saw Jesus and heard his voice, they fell back in some consternation; "this must be a mistake; this is not at all the kind of man we were told we were going to arrest". A second time, then, Jesus asks them, "for whom are you looking?" They reply as before; Jesus repeats, "I am he" and adds that if they are looking for him, they can let his companions go. The disciples, however, are not willing to be dismissed like this. There is a scuffle (only the Fourth Gospel mentions names); Peter draws his sword and wounds the high priest's servant, Malchus. Jesus says, "put your sword back into its sheath; the cup which my Father has given me – shall I not drink it?"

The arresting party may well have been warned that their work is to be done as secretly and quietly as possible, but the disciples, who were not cowards, will hardly have been willing to have their Master led off without an attempt to save him. The fact that there was only a scuffle, and that in spite of what Peter had done, the disciples were apparently left unmolested, and that they obeyed the command of Jesus and his obvious wish is a sidelight upon the majesty of his presence. There might so well have been an "ugly incident' with unpredictable consequences but for the power of Jesus' presence.

In the story that follows concerning the trial before the High Priest and Peter's tragic denial (vv. 12–27) there is a difficult textual problem upon which the learned commentaries may be consulted. It seems much best that we should accept the order of the verses as they are given in the Old Syriac version reading the verses in this order, 12, 13, 24, 14, 15, 19–23, 16–18, 26, 27. The reasons for thinking that the Syriac version gives us the correct order are these in brief: (1) The Greek word *'oun*, meaning 'therefore', at the beginning of v. 24 does not make good sense, (2) the editor has carefully told us that Caiaphas was High Priest that year (v. 13); it is extremely unlikely, therefore, that he would have called Annas High Priest in verse 19. (3) It is very unlikely that Peter who is said to have denied Christ before Annas (v. 17) would have moved on when Jesus was taken before Caiaphas and would then again have twice denied him (vv. 25 f.). If we take the story in the order of the Old Syriac, it is quite straightforward.

The temple police, then, arrest Jesus, bind him and bring him before Annas, the head of the priestly family, the high priesthood being held by Caiaphas in accordance with Roman demands, which had deposed Annas. Annas therefore passes him on to Caiaphas (v. 24). It was Caiaphas, it will be remembered, who had urged that Jesus, even though he were guilty of no offence which could be brought before the Roman courts, was a public danger and should be disposed of (v. 14).

When Jesus was taken before Caiaphas, John and Peter followed. John as an acquaintance of the High Priest, and therefore presumably known to his doorkeeper, was admitted to the hall, but Peter remained outside the door. Caiaphas questions Jesus about his followers and about his teaching. Jesus replies that all his teaching has been in public, sometimes in the synagogue, sometimes in the temple; there has been no secret teaching. If the High Priest wants to know what he has been saying, let him make public inquiry. At this point one of the high priest's servants gives Jesus a blow. "Is that the way to talk to the High Priest?" Jesus replies, "if I have spoken amiss, bring evidence of what is wrong. If my answer is a fair answer, why strike me?" (vv. 19–23).

Meanwhile John has managed to get Peter admitted to the hall, but the maid at the door, as she admits him, says, "aren't you one of this fellow's followers?" Peter says, "No, I am not". It was cold that night, and the servants were all gathered round the fire, Peter standing with them (vv. 16–18). While Peter was standing and warming himself others said to him, "surely you are one of his followers?" "No, I'm not", said Peter. Then one of the high priest's slaves, a relation of Malchus, said, "didn't I see you in the garden with him?", and again Peter said No. At that moment the cock crew (vv. 26 f.).

XVIII. 28–XIX. 30. Barrett claims that "most of the material" in this section from XVIII. 28–XIX. 16 is based on the Marcan narrative*. John II in that case was a novelist.

Jesus' condemnation by Caiaphas is a foregone conclusion. He

* op. cit. p. 443.

must be destroyed, but capital punishment was forbidden the Jews by the Romans except in the case of a Gentile found in the inner courts of the temple. As early as possible, therefore, when morning has come they bring Jesus to the procurator's residence. They will not go inside lest thereby they incur ceremonial defilement on the day of the Passover, for John knew, as the Synoptists did not, that the Last Supper was not on the Passover night but on the previous evening. Pilate courteously comes outside to see the delegation. "What charge have you against this man?" he asks. "If he had not been a scoundrel deserving of death," they reply, "we should not have brought him before you." "Take him and judge him for yourselves," says Pilate, "unless he has committed some offence with which my court is concerned." "But you have taken away our right of capital punishment", say his accusers. Pilate therefore went indoors and sent for Jesus to be brought before him.

At the interview between Jesus and Pilate John, we may be quite certain, was not present. Scholars have therefore supposed that the account of the interview given here is a product of the evangelist's imagination. There can be no proof or certainty in a matter of this kind. I would suggest, however, that this is an odd account for a novelist with a free hand to have produced. I do not suppose that the editor simply invented this dialogue; therefore presumably he got it from what he heard from John I in some form. Whence did John get it? It is at least possible that others were present, slaves perhaps or servants and officials, when Pilate interviewed Jesus. It is therefore at least possible that we have here a somewhat garbled account of what really happened.

Pilate asks Jesus directly, "are you the king of the Jews?" The interview can hardly have begun in a manner so abrupt, unless, as we must assume, Jesus' accusers had said something about his claiming to be a king. Jesus inquires whether Pilate is asking if Jesus himself claims to be the king of the Jews, or is Pilate merely referring to hearsay. Pilate seems to reply, "internal religious squabbles of the Jews are no concern of mine, but the authorities have brought you before me. What have you been up to that there is this sort of talk?" Jesus replies that he claims no earthly kingship at all. "So then, are you really a king of some sort?" asks Pilate. To this Jesus seems to have replied that 'kingship' was

148

Pilate's word, that for himself Jesus was not concerned with words but with reality. "What is reality?" asks Pilate.

Kingship may in some way have been discussed between Jesus and Pilate, and Pilate must have been convinced that no political question or claim was here involved. He had a contempt for the Jews; at the same time the Roman authorities were always anxious about outbreaks of mob excitement at the time of the great festivals. Pilate, therefore, goes out to the delegation waiting outside the residency and says to them, in effect, "I cannot find that this man is guilty of any offence that is any concern of mine, but I suggest a compromise. You know that we are accustomed as a special act of clemency to release one prisoner on this occasion; I propose to release this time this 'king of the Jews'." But the delegation shouted, "we don't want him; it's Barabbas we want!" Barabbas was just a brigand.

XIX. 1–16. Throughout this account of Jesus' trial before Pilate, the procurator shows supreme contempt for the Jewish people. On the other hand, he is very anxious to avoid trouble and mob violence when Jerusalem was crowded with visitors; moreover, he has no understanding at all of the person who stands before him. He had rather hoped to escape the troublesome matter by letting the notorious Barabbas free again, but this device had failed. No possible capital charge lies against Jesus, but the accused person has obviously been making trouble, and he might be taught a lesson. Pilate, it seems, hands over Jesus to be scourged, a usual custom of a Roman governor to extract fresh evidence. The soldiers flog him, set on his head a crown of thorns and wrap him in a garment of royal purple, knock him about and jeer at him (vv. 1–3). Pilate thereupon goes out again and says to the delegation, "I am bringing him out that you may know I find no case against him." Jesus is then brought out still wearing the crown of thorns and the purple robe, and Pilate says, "here he is" with the suggestion, "surely I have done all that I could be expected to do; be content with that". But the delegation shouts out, "we want him crucified". "Very well," says Pilate, "take him off and crucify him yourselves. I find no fault in him." Stung to greater fury by this the delegation says, "you know very well that we are not allowed to put men to death, but by our laws he ought to die because he has claimed to be a son of God". This apparently was the first definite charge made against Jesus by his accusers, and Pilate is considerably alarmed, presumably because the appearance of some religious pretender in the present crowded and excitable state of the city might cause great mischief; Pilate's business was to keep things quiet. (vv. 4–8).

He goes back into the Residency and has Jesus brought before him once again. "Where do you come from?" asks Pilate. It was by now almost midday; Jesus has had no sleep and must have been in a state of physical exhaustion; we may think, too, that he now saw that Pilate would give way to the Jewish importunity. To Pilate's question he makes no reply. "What do you mean by not answering my question," says Pilate in exasperation, "don't you realise that I have authority to set you free or to have you crucified?" "God gave you all the authority you have", said Jesus. Pilate, who had a Roman's respect for law, made, it seems, further efforts to avoid giving way to the Jewish accusers, but this word 'king' was a dangerous word; it smacked of treason. "If you let this man off," they said in effect, "we shall let the emperor know that you have tolerated treason." Pilate therefore has Jesus brought outside the Residency once again; set him on the throne,* and mockingly says to the Jews, "Here's your king!" It was midday (XV. 25). They in dreadful treason to their religious heritage and their own private feelings shout out, "we recognise no king but the emperor". Pilate thereupon gave way and ordered that Jesus should be crucified (vv. 9–15).

XIX. 17–22. Our difficulty in the sheltered western world is to realise that this actually happened, that it happened to him whose life and teaching previous chapters have expounded, and that a not wholly dissimilar fate has overtaken and still overtakes thousands of relatively innocent people. The crucifixion of Jesus is a typical event in history.

Jesus, then, is led out to the place called Golgotha carrying the cross-piece for his crucifixion. He was fastened on the cross with

---

* Or, perhaps more probably, "sat himself on the throne". The verb could be either transitive or intransitive.

two criminals, one on each side of him. Pilate had no understanding of Jesus, but he had great contempt for the Jews, and to have the last word and as a grim joke he had "Jesus of Nazareth the King of the Jews" inscribed on Jesus' cross in three languages. There were indignant protests of course, but Pilate would not remove the offending notice, "what I have written, I have written", a superb instance of what the Greeks called irony, for Pilate had written so much more truly than he knew.

XIX. 23–30. The clothes of those crucified were treated by the soldiers as their perquisites. Four persons are mentioned as being present, Jesus' Mother and his aunt with Mary, the wife of Clopas, and Mary of Magdala. The disciples were presumably present in the crowd and certainly John, for Jesus even in his death agony does not forget his Mother and commends her to John's care and keeping. Then Jesus says, "I'm thirsty." There was a jar of vinegar there. Someone filled a sponge with it and lifted it to his mouth on a javelin.* Then Jesus said, "it is finished"; his head fell forward and he was dead.

* The word 'hyssopos' may well be a mistake for a shorter word 'hyssos' meaning a javelin.

I HAVE worked out, as best I could, my hypothesis or guess and may be permitted in the end to comment on it.

I have worked, in particular, upon two assumptions, first that Jesus of Nazareth was a real human being. That was never doubted by those amongst whom he moved. The Jesus of the Fourth Gospel is the risen and ascended Lord of the Church's faith; this Jesus is represented under the forms of an historical narrative, but, as is plain from internal contradictions and from the Synoptic Gospels, the Fourth Gospel, as it stands, is unhistorical.

But, second, I have assumed that John II, as I have called him, wrote in all good faith; he selected his material so as to set forth his great theological theme; he has told his story in his own way and in his own terms of glowing faith, but he did not consciously invent. His picture of Jesus rests upon current oral (or possibly written) traditions about him and more particularly, as I have supposed, upon the reminiscences of John I. It has been my effort in every section to guess what John I may have so said that it would be written or translated by John II into the form in which we have it.

In respect of every particular section neither I nor any reader could say more than that events *may* indeed so have occurred, or Jesus *may* so have spoken, but I find the sum total of my reconstruction much more nearly convincing than any part of it. When I began my attempt, I had little idea what I should find. What in the end I have found, as it seems to me, is a portrait of Jesus which most certainly I did not invent, a portrait that is entirely consistent with the picture of him in the Synoptic Gospels but at the same time very notably different from it, a more intimate or contemporary portrait. Moreover – and I would lay much stress upon this – if Jesus was such as I have supposed John I to have portrayed him, he was indeed a human being but one of such gigantic spiritual stature that we can begin to understand how Paul and

153

the author of *Hebrews* and of the *Revelation* came to write, as they do, of one who lived and died in the contemporary world they knew.

First we see Jesus at the time of his baptism making a profound impression on the Baptist who points him out to some of his followers as one with a deeper insight than his own. Thus there naturally gathers a little company drawn to him, Andrew, Peter, Philip, Nathanael and presumably John I himself. There follows the strange story of the turning of the water into wine, which I have treated, not as a fairy story nor a rehashed myth, but as an historical event intelligibly twisted in folk memory. John II, concerned as an artist to draw a picture of the majestic Lord of the Church's faith, was not interested in chronology; there follows, therefore, the story of the cleansing of the temple, which in our eyes much more clearly than the Cana story reveals the compelling presence, the power, the "glory" of "the man Christ Jesus". Jesus is asked by what authority he has so acted; he replies, it seems, that if the temple with all its accoutrements and rituals disappeared from the earth, he by the manifestation of the power of God would soon raise up a spiritual temple for the worship of the spiritual God.

The story of Nicodemus I have taken to be based upon a real conversation between Jesus and a serious inquirer. Jesus says to him, in effect, that unless we become as humble and open-minded as children we cannot enter the kingdom of heaven. Next comes the conversation with the woman of Samaria; this is either pure fiction, in which case John II has remarkable gifts as a romantic writer, or it is based on an historical event. I have taken the latter view that we have, in Johannine rewriting, an account of a personal and apparently chance interview between Jesus and a woman of no reputation who again and again tries to parry his words and is forced at last to face his challenge. The second 'sign' or miracle that Jesus did in Galilee was the healing of the officer's son. If we no longer regard this as a 'miracle', it points to a remarkable psychic or spiritual sensitivity in Jesus, which we can well believe. Another healing follows, that of the sick man at the pool of Bethesda on the Sabbath day (vv. 1–18). In the controversy that arises Jesus both reasserted his assurance of his mission and vindicated his understanding of the Sabbath day.

154

The feeding of the five thousand (VI. 1–15) and the walking on the water (VI. 16–21) I have rationalised but treated as events marking a crisis in the ministry of Jesus and have suggested that on the following Sabbath he spoke in the synagogue in Capernaum upon the heavenly manna which in the name and power of the Father he was offering to men. Again his authority is challenged, and again he makes no claim for himself except that like the prophets he was sent. He, however, was sent not merely to declare the word of God but to bring to men the bread from heaven. He offers, he challenges, he demands decision. In two ways he has now offended national pride; he has refused to become a national leader against the Romans and has declared that it is not enough to claim descent from Abraham. At this point a large part of his following deserts him; the few, puzzled but strangely moved, stand by him still.

The Feast of Tabernacles is at hand (Ch. VII). We hear the crowd discussing him; is he a good man or a charlatan, will he venture up to the feast, and what will happen if he does? In the middle of the feast Jesus appears in the temple and expounds the Scriptures. There is much excitement. The authorities send to arrest him, but for the moment he escapes. On the last day of the feast, when the water is ceremonially brought from Shiloah to the temple, Jesus speaks in the temple of the real, the true, the heavenly water of life and bids the people accept him and his message and partake of the heavenly provision now. Throughout this scene we catch the voice of the crowd and the challenge of the solitary and majestic, imperious and yet pleading voice of Jesus.

The story of the woman taken in adultery, interpolated into the text of this Gospel, I have taken for history. It vividly brings home to us the awe-inspiring presence of Jesus; the excited mob that dragged the poor woman before him could not face his eye; one by one they slunk away. (VII. 53–VIII. 11.) There follows (VIII. 12–20) a long Johannine discourse in which Jesus is represented as the Light of the World. The discourse, as it stands, is wholly unhistorical, but I have shown that though Jesus made no claims for himself in fact and appeared before men "in great humility", yet with unmistakable authority, it was implied in his teaching and his mission that he was the Light of the World; John II has not misrepresented what he taught. In VIII. 12–59 beneath an extended Johannine narrative we see Jesus insisting that it is a matter of life and death to men whether or not they obey his word; he is going away; he has only a little time left with them; now they must decide. We overhear the response and protests and questions of the crowd. What is this new teaching that it is not enough to be children of Abraham, the chosen? We feel the tension of the scene: either this man is mad, or he is a prophet of God; this is a matter about which one may not keep an open mind.

IX. 1–41. The healing of the blind man is followed once again by the questioning of his authority. In X. 1–21 we have a parable or perhaps two parables of Jesus retranslated into Johannine terms, and then a vivid scene in Solomon's porch where Jesus is nearly lynched and in the end is nearly arrested but escapes.

I have again rationalised the story of the raising of Lazarus, but have treated it as an historical event. It seems that Jesus may have made a mistake thinking that Lazarus was dead. The miracle, as it was deemed to be, leads to Caiaphas's demand that at all costs Jesus be got rid of. There follow the stories of the anointing at Bethany and then of the Passion.

The picture of Jesus that emerges is that of the same figure whom the Synoptists depict, but it is a very different portrait. The incidents narrated are, for the most part, different and the teaching is, so to put it, evangelical rather than ethical.

Modern scholars have taught us to distinguish clearly between *didache* and *kerugma*, that is, between teaching and the proclamation of the preacher. The Synoptists represent, in the main, *didache* or Jesus as the Teacher; John I presents us with Jesus the Evangelist who is the Evangel, the Good News, in his own person. He appears as a commanding and imperial figure of a controlled and burning ardour, who, for all his compassion and understanding, brings a sword, not peace, speaking less as Teacher than as Prophet with the assured sense that God was visiting the world through him, that to reject him was to reject the voice of God. Yet was he of an infinite compassion especially for the outcast, the needy, the neglected, incarnating in himself the divine good will and compassion of the Father which he proclaimed. From this Gospel we should know little of his teaching about God and the kingdom; it is not his words but himself that is revealed. None ever spoke as this man, none ever was as he in the magnificence of his courage, in his utter faith in God, in his infinite compassion for those to whom he spoke.

He went to his death trusting that God would vindicate the word that he had spoken. We are presented with the same dilemma as those who heard his voice and saw his eye – is he mad, or is he indeed the way, the truth, the life? There is no demonstrable answer unless proof lie in this that as many as have received him to them he has given power to become the sons of God; they have known from their own experience that "this is eternal life to know thee, the only true God and Jesus Christ whom thou hast sent".